Religion in Antebellum Kentucky

JOHN B. BOLES

THE UNIVERSITY PRESS OF KENTUCKY

Research for The Kentucky Bicentennial Bookshelf
is assisted by a grant from the
National Endowment for the Humanities.
Views expressed in the Bookshelf do not
necessarily represent those of the Endowment.

ISBN: 0-8131-0227-8

Library of Congress Catalog Card Number: 76-4434

A statewide cooperative scholarly publishing agency
serving Berea College, Centre College of Kentucky,
Eastern Kentucky University, Georgetown College,
Kentucky Historical Society, Kentucky State University,
Morehead State University, Murray State University,
Northern Kentucky University, Transylvania University,
University of Kentucky, University of Louisville, and
Western Kentucky University.

Editorial and Sales Offices: Lexington, Kentucky 40506

For David Christopher

Contents

Preface

THIS BRIEF BOOK is an introduction to the religious history of antebellum Kentucky, though I have tried to place the account within the context of southern history in general. Because of severe limitations of space, I have discussed only those religious groups sizable enough to have a significant impact on Kentucky. For example, even though Louis Brandeis was born in Louisville in 1856, the Jewish community there was too limited in size to merit treatment. On the other hand, I have tried to go beyond mere narrative and be interpretative when the material and my ability permitted. The result, I hope, will be useful both to the general reader and more specialized students of religion and the South. A longer, footnoted typescript of the book is deposited at the Maryland Historical Society.

Even in a short book an author incurs numerous debts. My colleagues and students have offered encouragement, and all those with heavy teaching loads know how important that can be. Several scholars have read individual chapters, and to them I express sincere appreciation: the Reverend Vincent Eaton, Philip Gleason, the Reverend Vincent P. McMurry, and Willie Lee Rose. Chapter 5 was presented at the Homewood Seminar in American Religious History at the Johns Hopkins University; I am indebted to Timothy L. Smith for giving me this valuable opportunity. The library staffs of the Maryland Historical Society and Towson State College were unfailingly cooperative. Moreover, a grant from the college expedited the early research. Mary Bowersox expertly typed the manuscript. My wife, Nancy, was invaluable, reading each draft several times and insisting upon clarity of expression. She also helped with that most dreary of tasks, proofreading. Our son David, to whom the book is dedicated, was a joyful distraction throughout the entire process of research and writing.

1

THE PLANTING

THE "DARK AND BLOODY GROUND" was the Indian name
for that beautiful territory which began in mountains on
the western edge of Virginia, gently sloped west, and
declined to the Mississippi River. For countless moons
Cherokees and Iroquois battled incessantly for the land,
giving the region its martial name. The same qualities of
fertility and abundant game that attracted the Indians also
caught the attention of the competing French and English, and for almost a century after LaSalle discovered the
falls near present-day Louisville in 1669, the two European rivals cast longing eyes at Kentucky. Two years later
a party of Virginians sent west by their governor, Sir
William Berkeley, traversed the region. But then for
almost eighty years, except for anonymous trappers and
possibly Indian kidnap victims (and a French explorer
who happened upon Big Bone Lick in 1739), no Euro-
peans vied for the land. Suddenly there was a flurry of
activity. Celeron de Bienville in 1749 visited the future
state and even buried lead plates to assure the legitimacy
of France's claim, but it was the arrival the following year
of Dr. Thomas Walker and Christopher Gist, coming
separately and for different land companies in the English colonies, that began the onrush of English-American
exploration and eventually settlement. From their travels
grandiose tales of the land west of the mountains

emerged, and soon other adventurers caught the fever. John Findley's descriptions seized the fancy of Daniel Boone, and the western urge never left him. After Boone's celebrated travels opened new vistas for American pioneers already heady with visions of luxuriant soils and forests crowded with deer, the great American trek westward began in earnest. Kentucky was to be the first state carved out of the wilderness west of the Appalachians.

John Filson, one of Kentucky's most famous publicists, described the region in 1784 as "the most extraordinary country that the sun enlightens with his celestial beams," and in an Appendix to his *Kentucke* he introduced colonial readers to "Col. Daniel Boon." Boone's narrative, refracted no doubt through the promotional prose of Filson, portrayed with feigned amazement: "Thus we behold Kentucke, lately an howling wilderness, the habitation of savages and wild beasts, become a fruitful field." Extravagant praise of the new territory trickled back to avid listeners in Virginia especially. Who would not be eager to brave the rigors of the distance, pass through that wonderful natural gateway, the Cumberland Gap, and behold a better tomorrow? And even in that new land toward the sunset, the comforting and civilizing forces of religion would be felt. As Boone himself rhapsodized, "Here, where the hand of violence shed the blood of the innocent, where the horrid yells of savages, and the groans of the distressed, sounded in our ears, we now hear the praises and adorations of our Creator."

Kentucky entered the Union in 1792 as the fifteenth state, but for two decades rival land companies, led by trailblazers and would-be impresarios, had laid claim to Bluegrass empires. James Harrod in early 1774 built cabins and later a fort; thus at "Harrodsburg" began the first permanent white settlement in Kentucky. The following year Judge Richard Henderson, dreaming imperial dreams as head of the Transylvania Company, called delegates from the then four Kentucky settlements to meet together near a fort that Daniel Boone was completing by the Kentucky River—eventually the town of Boonesborough. The delegates assembled, and because there was no building to hold them, they met in a small meadow bordering a stream called Spring Link, which opened into the Kentucky River. This historic plain, then covered with a blanket of white clover, had in its center a huge elm tree whose circumference of shade Judge Henderson estimated to be 400 feet. Under the canopy of foliage was organized, May 23–27, 1775, the proprietary government for the proposed Transylvania Colony. One of the Harrodsburg delegates was an Anglican minister, the Reverend John Lyth, and on May 28, the Sunday following the establishment of the trans-Appalachian government, beneath the arms of that majestic elm tree, the first public service of worship was held in Kentucky. In the shade of the "church tree" were heard prayers for England's "most gracious sovereign Lord King George." The American Revolution soon ended prayers for royalty, but at least a portion of Daniel Boone's prophecy turns out to be true: on the frontier now sounded "the praises and adorations of our Creator."

From this auspicious beginning, one might have expected substantial Anglican or Episcopal growth, but history is unpredictable. In a state whose early queen city was named after the revolutionary battle at Lexington, the Church of England had an unpopular tradition to overcome. Consequently the stately Church of England made but faltering progress in the new frontier state. The Episcopal church had more than its Tory reputation to live down. During the Revolution the denomination almost folded, and after the war the disorganized group was so preoccupied with trying to establish a new ecclesiastical structure that it simply could not concern itself with missions in Kentucky. Finally in 1789 the Diocese of Maryland sent word that one of its sons, the Reverend William Duke, was emigrating to the Bluegrass. Illness struck Duke, however, near Harper's Ferry, and he returned to an active clerical career in Maryland.

Certainly there were individuals scattered across the varied terrain of Kentucky who identified themselves as Episcopalian, but for these adherents there was no church. In the vicinity of Lexington in the early 1790s a group of such citizens, calling themselves the "Episcopal Society," met for informal services at a nearby farm. In their midst was a young Presbyterian graduate from Washington College in Virginia, James Moore, who taught classics at the local Transylvania Seminary. Moore intended to wear the cloth as a Presbyterian, but his independence of views and steadfast refusal to withdraw sections of two sermons preached as part of his ordination examination caused the synod to dismiss him. Dismayed yet not persuaded to modify his beliefs, young Moore adamantly pursued the ministry. Meeting the Episcopal Society in Lexington, he was pleasantly surprised to discover their religious views were compatible with his. Moreover, they were impressed with him. Consequently Moore returned to Virginia, was ordained by Bishop James Madison, and in 1794 returned to Lexington as an Episcopal minister. Two years later an Episcopal church was organized in Lexington in a ramshackle frame house on the site of the present-day Christ Church.

As so often was the case, Moore had a strong commitment to education, and after his church was under way he accepted two part-time academic positions, the presidency of Kentucky Academy in Pisgah, eight miles southwest of Lexington, and of Transylvania Seminary in Lexington. When these two institutions merged in 1799 to become Transylvania University, Moore became its president and professor of logic, metaphysics, moral philosophy, and belles-lettres. Even with heavy teaching and administrative duties Moore continued as rector of his growing church. Such multiple responsibilities were burdensome and gave the rector no time to spread his faith beyond Lexington. He and his congregation sent pleading letters to several of the eastern bishops, and again it was the Diocese of Maryland, not Virginia, who recognized the need. Bishop Thomas Clagget promptly commissioned the Reverend Samuel Keene, Jr., a missionary to Kentucky.

For nine months Keene was stationed in Lexington and with Christian zeal and joy preached the Episcopal message in the neighboring towns, especially Georgetown, Winchester, and Paris, helping to organize scattered small congregations. Near Lexington, Keene met an able young Methodist itinerant, the Reverend Williams Kavanaugh, whom he persuaded to take Episcopal orders. Since the Methodist church had been separate from the Episcopal only fifteen years, this required no great theological readjustment, and Kavanaugh went to Baltimore, was examined, and on June 20, 1800, became an ordained Episcopal priest. Returning to Lexington, Kavanaugh served as James Moore's assistant while Moore was laying the educational foundations for Transylvania's brief greatness as a university. With the close of the century, the Episcopal church finally had a sure toehold in Kentucky, but it was only a toehold. Not until 1820, when George Thomas Chapman was named rector of the parish in Lexington, did the Episcopal faith come of age in Kentucky.

Although there had long been a variety of Baptists in the South, the denomination really took root after 1755 when Shubal Stearns and Daniel Marshall emigrated from Connecticut to North Carolina, carrying with them their fervent and evangelical Separate Baptist faith. By the 1760s Separate Baptist churches were sparking great Baptist growth in both North Carolina and Virginia despite persecution from the established Church of England. At this time the various kinds of Baptists—Particular (believing in strict Calvinism and adhering to the Philadelphia Confession of Faith), General (believing salvation was open to everyone who desires it), and Separate (evangelical, Calvinistic, but accepting no creed other than the Bible)—often feuded. Perhaps it was to escape this theological bickering and the possible persecution from Anglicans, in addition to desiring bountiful fertile land, which led so many Virginia Baptists to transplant themselves to Kentucky. Once there, many tried to neutralize their previous divisions by calling themselves Regular Baptists, though a Separate Baptist stronghold did develop south of the Kentucky River. Estimates have suggested that as many as one-quarter of all Virginia Baptists came to Kentucky.

Squire Boone, Daniel's brother, was a Baptist minister, but it is not known if he preached in Kentucky. The first Baptist sermons appear to have been delivered by Thomas Tinsley who initially preached in Harrodsburg in April 1776. The next year William Hickman began exhorting the Baptist faithful, followed in the coming few years by such pioneer Baptists as Joseph Reading, John Taylor, and William Marshall. Clearly many of the earliest Kentucky settlers were Baptist in sentiment, though they seemed more interested in land claims and house raisings than the sacraments. Within five short years, however, in 1781, under a sugar maple tree near present-day Elizabethtown, the Severns Valley Baptist Church was organized, with services usually held in hospitable cabins by the Reverend John Gerrard. Meanwhile, another Baptist church, Cedar Creek, had been organized in Nelson County on July 4, 1781. But far away in Virginia events were transpiring at a local church that symbolized the attraction Kentucky had for Old Dominion Baptists.

Upper Spotsylvania Baptist Church, organized in Orange County, Virginia, in 1767, was the first Separate Baptist church north of the James River. Since 1770 its minister had been Lewis Craig who, after visiting Kentucky in 1779 and perhaps again in 1780, caught the migration fever. He could not get those visions of rich virgin soil out of his mind, and slowly he came to envision a church migration that to him paralleled the people of

Israel leaving Egypt for the promised Canaan. Land grants in distant Kentucky were obtained as family after family decided to follow their pastor and church across the mountains. Slowly the Baptist entourage took shape, with Captain William Ellis, who had been in Kentucky with Boone in 1770, as their guide and military leader. Farewell Sunday came in September 1781 as hundreds gathered round the church, their wagons loaded, dogs barking, babies crying. From a makeshift stand beside the church Craig gave the group a moving sermon, sketching the recent growth of Virginia Baptists in the face of oppressive laws and portraying the sure liberty and "il-limitable acres of a western Canaan" where surely God was leading them. Hardly an eye was dry, and all hearts were astir at the close of this valedictory. Early the next morning, to the creaking of heavily laden wagons and the shouts of drivers, the Baptist caravan (200 church members, perhaps 500–600 in all) was on its way, carrying the minutes, communion set, and an old Bible from Spotsylvania. The "Traveling Church" was moving west.

None could foresee accurately the sheer drudgery, even the anguish, of such a long and adventurous journey. Dust made breathing difficult, rain pelted the sojourners, cold winds cut through coats and blankets. Nature some-times seemed to conspire with the Indians and human weariness to discourage the settlers, but they trudged onward, crossing the Blue Ridge through Bedford's Gap. Finally after what must have seemed like an interminable autumn the Traveling Church passed through the Cum-berland Gap and entered Kentucky about the first of December 1781. The life of the church—preaching, prayers, hymn singing, baptisms—continued along the way, Craig leading his flock assisted by "Uncle Peter," a slave preacher owned by Craig, who presented the gospel to the accompanying slaves. Craig kept the image of the "Israelitish wandering" before them, reminding them that beyond the mountains lay the Promised Land.

7

By the second Sunday of December they reached Gilbert's Creek, in what is now Garrard County, and there settled temporarily. A clearing was made, a stockade was erected for protection against the Indians, cabins were hastily built, and atop a hill a sturdy log church, with loop-holes for guns, was quickly completed. With the old familiar Bible and communion set at hand, the congregation gathered together under roof for the first time in the strange new land. Craig continued to travel about, preaching to far-flung impromptu congregations in Kentucky. Captain Ellis had already moved beyond Gilbert's Creek to settle on the magnificent land in the Bluegrass region, and soon Craig and others from the Traveling Church saw there still greener pastures. In the early fall Craig and most of his congregation once again picked up their belongings, took to the primitive roads, and reconstituted themselves the South Elkhorn Baptist Church in a new location, about five miles from Lexington. Soon the Kentucky Baptists were enjoying a slow but steady growth.

Early in the eighteenth century Scotch-Irish Presbyterians from Pennsylvania had moved south down the broad Valley of Virginia and into the Piedmont regions of Virginia and both Carolinas. By the Revolution the states south of the Mason-Dixon line had been organized into synods and presbyteries, the ecclesiastical governing bodies of the Presbyterians. Before statehood Kentucky was the western territory of Virginia, and as Virginians traveled westward into the heralded Kentucky, slowly and almost imperceptibly numerous individual Presbyterians came to call the former haunt of warring Indians their own home. In 1780 Terah Templin, a young Presbyterian licensed to preach but not yet ordained by Hanover Presbytery in Virginia, conducted the first Presbyterian services in Kentucky, but no churches were founded.

Three years later, during the year that saw the American Revolution concluded by treaty, an able Virginia

Presbyterian divine, David Rice, visited Kentucky looking for land bargains to support his expanding family. While there he preached to the Presbyterian settlers hungry for the sermons and worship services they loved and missed. Returning to his home and church at Peaks of Otter, Bedford County, Virginia, he fully expected to finish out his life in his home state. Yet Rice had so invigorated those pioneer Presbyterians in Kentucky, many of whom had previously known him in Virginia, that in the late summer of 1783 they sent to him a subscription list signed by 300, detailing their religious destitution and entreating him to serve God by serving them in the West. Moved by this demonstration of support and remembering the bountiful land by which he could more adequately provide for his family, Rice took the petition to his supervisory body, the Hanover Presbytery, and got official permission to plant Presbyterianism beyond the mountains.

Father Rice, as he was called, was clearly the outstanding religious leader of early Kentucky. Born in Hanover County, Virginia, in 1733, he was converted by the famous Samuel Davies and educated at Nassau Hall (Princeton). An eminent clergyman, David Rice left the comfortable confines of Virginia for the challenge of frontier Kentucky. After arriving at Danville in October 1783, Rice during the winter months was restricted by the impassable roads to the immediate vicinity, but with spring he expanded his field of labors in central Kentucky. Within a year Rice had organized the first three Presbyterian congregations in Kentucky: Concord in Danville, Cane Run near Harrodsburg, and New Providence on the Salt River.

Like so many Presbyterian ministers, Rice combined teaching with his ministry, soon opening a school in his Kentucky home. Independent of his arrival, Virginia (Kentucky was still a county of the Old Dominion) incorporated the Transylvania Seminary in 1783, authorized a board of trustees, and provided land grants totaling

9

12,000 acres as endowment for the school. Because his Princeton degree was a rarity in a frontier society and because he was eminent and of good character, David Rice was elected chairman of the board on February 1, 1785, and in 1787 the infant seminary of learning opened in his home. The following year the seminary, then more a grammar school than a college, moved to Lexington and after a succession of presidencies achieved great stature within a generation.

As an indication of Rice's position, he was chosen a delegate to the convention which met at Danville in 1792 to frame a state constitution. There he argued nobly but in vain for a provision authorizing the gradual abolition of slavery. Shortly before this occasion he had published, under the pseudonym "Philanthropos," a bombshell: *Slavery Inconsistent with Justice and Good Policy* (Philadelphia, 1792), the first blow against the institution struck by a clergyman west of the Appalachians and the beginning of a long struggle by a minority element in western religion to eliminate slavery. It was a mark of Rice's towering reputation that he could prominently lead such a fight and remain a popular, even venerated minister, "the Father of Kentucky Presbyterianism." Under his leadership Transylvania Presbytery was organized in 1786, and Presbyterianism had a foundation from which gradual progress could be made. But until a group of younger, more evangelical ministers joined Rice and his co-workers, Kentucky Presbyterianism remained small in numbers yet influential out of proportion to size.

The Methodist faith that experienced phenomenal growth in the nineteenth century was late to begin in America and still later in Kentucky. Organized Methodism arrived in America in 1766, and by 1773 Robert Williams had brought the torch to southeastern Virginia where an evangelistic Anglican, the Reverend Devereux Jarratt, ignited a Methodist revival of far-reaching significance. Soon Virginia was the Methodist stronghold in America. Yet Methodists were stung during the Revolution by John Wesley's—and by implication their—Toryism. Wesley recognized after the war that American Methodism had to be given independence too, so at his direction Methodist delegates met in Baltimore at the famous "Christmas Conference" of December 1784. The Methodist Episcopal church was born, headed for more than thirty years by the indefatigable Francis Asbury. A sophisticated organization was established by which itinerant ministers traveled over broad circuits, thereby reaching more people than they could have otherwise. To keep discipline intact and zeal aflame during the minister's absence, classes and "bands" of pious laymen were formed to watch over one another. With this kind of structure, perfectly suited to the frontier where the population was often too sparse for traditionally organized churches, Methodism flourished.

In the migration of Virginians westward were many Methodists. In early 1783 the Reverend Francis Clark and an experienced class leader, John Durham, moved from Virginia and settled near Danville. Because he was one of the few Methodist ministers who were married, Clark preached from one station; he was what was termed a "local preacher." Clark's ministry produced the first Methodist society in Kentucky. Soon other local preachers called Kentucky their home: William J. Thompson from North Carolina, Thomas Stevenson from Maryland. But these stationary preachers could not keep pace with the rapid population growth, and in 1786, at Bishop Asbury's direction, a Kentucky Circuit was added to the Methodist organization. Two missionaries, James Haw and Benjamin Ogden, were sent into the new territory to ride the first circuits there. Finding groups of Methodist individuals organized into "societies," these two itinerants began harvesting the fruit of the religious seeds sowed by the local preachers. Methodism had been planted in Kentucky, although its first fifteen years offered little hope for much growth. Asbury on his first visit to Kentucky in 1790 confided to his diary, "The Methodists do but little here—others lead the way." Real growth did not come until after 1800.

The Baptists, Methodists, and Presbyterians were to be the dominant denominations in early Kentucky, though there were scattered persons of other faiths, particularly Catholics and Episcopalians. In the years following their establishment in Kentucky, each of the major denominations slowly gained new ministers, organized additional churches, and watched their membership grow and then spurt during the Great Revival at the opening of the nineteenth century.

Most Kentuckians had left their relatives, neighbors, and familiar places in the seaboard states, and a nagging homesickness proved difficult to dismiss. In many parts of Kentucky the population was so scattered that loneliness was a major concern. Daniel Drake spoke of the "social bereavement" that plagued his family, a condition that recalls Henry Adams's remark that more menacing than the danger of Indians was "depressing homesickness, or the misery of nervous prostration, which wore out generation after generation of women and children on the frontier, and left a tragedy in every log-cabin." Some rugged individuals may have thrived on this isolation. Legend tells of Daniel Boone's desire for elbow room, and history records the story of Levi Harrod, a staunch Baptist pioneer, who left Kentucky for central Ohio because the settlers were getting so thick he could no longer get his "fresh b'ar meat." But most found the monotonous loneliness to be almost numbing and treasured the feeling of community and brotherhood offered by the churches. The old homesites in Virginia or Maryland could not be recovered, nor could old friends be gathered, but religious congregations did minister to nostalgic longings. Churches bound people together into close-knit spiritual families and as such performed a much-needed service for the mobile population.

Unbroken stretches of forest separated towns and settlements; since most trails and roads were unmarked, some itinerant ministers carried a small marking iron, about six inches long, to notch their private road-signs into obliging trees. Nevertheless ministers got lost, like the Methodist preacher Wilson Lee who in the summer of 1788 spent a frightening night alone in the forest. Indians still lurked in the shadows, protecting their villages and hunting grounds, and as late as 1790 a group of Presbyterians returning from worship was attacked, suffering two casualties. Sickness, death, and danger were constant companions to the first settlers, making the security and peace offered by religion a precious commodity.

The people carving their homes out of what Daniel Boone called a "howling wilderness" were on the whole not a sophisticated lot. As one rather snobbish Marylander wrote to his sister, "The Society of [Tennessee] is about on a par with Kentucky, some few genteel families and the rest mere clod hoppers—." Such a statement, if not untrue, was not quite fair. Schools were few and books almost nonexistent, but the religious leaders coped as best they could. The Presbyterian clergy often opened schools in their homes, and every itinerant Methodist had a saddlebag filled with devotional literature and other wholesome reading. In the absence of libraries a conference of Presbyterians meeting at Cane Run Church on July 12, 1785, recommended that collections be taken up and books be purchased to equip a simple theological lending library to accommodate the clergy and ministerial students. The ministers tried to adjust to the needs and abilities of the people. The manufacture and especially the consumption of whiskey on the frontier was, by our standards, extraordinary. Ministers—all except the Methodists—thought nothing of having a friendly drink with their fellowmen. The subscription list whereby members of a congregation agreed to help pay their minister's salary shows that money was almost unheard of. Baptist John Shackelford, pastor of the South Elkhorn Baptist Church in 1798, was promised 35 shillings along with 12.5 pounds of salt, 12.5 barrels of corn, 3 bushels of wheat, 363 pounds of pork, 100 pounds of flour, 100 pounds of beef, and 36 gallons of whiskey. If Shackelford collected, he was lucky; due to what colorful Peter Cartwright called "this parsimonious leprosy," many ministers never got paid in full. Moreover, the scattered settlements required the Baptist and sometimes the Presbyterian ministers to become at least part-time itinerants. Riding horseback over lonely roads, facing the fury of nature's elements, with little time for study and none for rest, usually woefully underpaid, the itinerants' duties, in Cartwright's phrase, "tried men's souls and bodies too."

Sturdy men with tough constitutions were essential for this ministry, and the Methodists and Baptists produced solid preachers who had risen from the backcountry folk to whom they preached. No separate clerical class of learned, aristocratic divines, these were men of the common people preaching an increasingly democratic faith. They could not parse Greek, but they could ride horseback, shoot, chew and spit tobacco, fight with the best of their parishioners, and if rowdies dared to disrupt a service, these ministers could apply a muscular Christianity to secure order. The sermons of the self-taught Baptists and Methodists were simple if long; those of the Presbyterians were more scholarly, as befits those who had at least some formal learning and an acquaintance with the classical languages. The Baptists and Methodists were especially effective among the plain folk because they spoke their language. As one less successful Baptist minister asked another, "Bro. Petty, how is it that the people like your preaching so much, and think so little of mine, when we both preach the same doctrine?" "Because," replied Petty, "I cut mine up so that they can eat it, while you give them yours whole." Preaching for long stretches in the raw open air, the revival ministers developed a peculiar sing-song style that was easier on their vocal cords. Exhorters were used at the close of sermons to apply with special fervor the call for salvation, and these exhorters often used all the magic that emotion and intensity could summon. Learned critics might sarcastically speak of being "gorged with the hum-drum balderdash nonsense of Baptistical preachers," but these ministers with a saddle for their study made converts, built churches, and spread Christianity across the face of the West.

So attracted were the Kentucky plain folk to this kind of preaching and the welcome camaraderie of the congregation that whole families walked or rode miles, dressed in their Sunday best, for the religious, social, and community highlight of the week, Sunday preaching. When it was time for the services to begin, the worshipers went into a log building that at most was twenty-five to thirty feet wide and perhaps forty to sixty feet long. There were no pews, simply pine boards or slabs on legs, without backs. The women sat on one side, the men on the other, and the blacks sat either at the back or in a gallery. There was no fireplace, very few windows, and a rude pulpit raised slightly from the floor. In the winter many people used hot bricks wrapped in cloth to keep their feet warm, but the dread of hellfire probably helped most forget the cold. Sermons were lengthy, and when combined with prayers and hymns, worship services were often two or three hours long. Families brought their Sunday dinners and after worship ate with friends and kin. Children scampered, youths courted, women talked of babies and cooking, men discussed crops and the weather. Then came time to journey home, and friends said their goodbyes and returned to their separate cabins, perhaps stopping on the way for neighborly visits. Sundays were a welcome relief from the toil and loneliness of frontier life.

2

THE HARVEST

B<small>Y THE MID</small>-1780s the denominations that were destined to play the dominant role in Kentucky's religious life were established in the territory. None could foresee the future course of history, yet many must have confidently accepted John Filson's remark of 1784 as predictive: "From these early movements it is hoped that Kentucky will eminently shine in learning and piety, which will fulfill the wish of every virtuous citizen." History, however, has an uncanny way of escaping the snares of those who try to confine it to the expected. And though Kentucky's population and commerce boomed in the fifteen years before 1800, religion appeared moribund. Rich and ample soils, a temperate climate, natural waterways guaranteed the new territory a future pregnant with greatness, but would the early premonitions of religion result only in a stillbirth? Church growth lagged far behind population; denominational bickering dispirited those relatively few who persevered in their faith. The orgy of speculation and boosterism, combined with a heritage of deism and indifference carried over from the Revolution, threatened to sweep away the early outposts of religion. In retrospect it is clear the forces of irreligion were not as powerful as contemporaries believed, and the religious footings were much firmer than they dared suspect. Yet what people believe to be true motivates human behavior, and the widespread worry that religion was collapsing had far-reaching implications.

When one reads the religious literature of the South in general as well as Kentucky for the 1790s, the overwhelming impression is one of religious depression. Peter Cartwright in his autobiography reported that Logan County, Kentucky, where he grew up, was a "rogue's harbor" with Sundays given over to every kind of entertainment but no religion. A 1794 letter from Kentucky to a famous English Baptist informed him "with concern—that religion appears to be at a very low ebb with every denomination in the State." A Methodist itinerant, traveling near Lexington in the autumn of 1795, feared that "the Universalists, joining with the Deists, had given Christianity a deadly stab hereabouts." And the Transylvania Presbytery as late as October 8, 1800, reveals in its minutes that its members were apprehensive about the "prevalence of vice and infidelity, the great apparent decline of true vital religion in too many places."

There were many reasons for this view of the era. It was an age of political challenge: the American Constitution had been ratified in 1789, and Kentucky amid many political differences had become a state in 1792. Then came the clamor caused by the threat of war with the Indians and with France, followed by the partisan Alien and Sedition Acts, and secular concerns distracted many people from religion. Kentucky was filling up with settlers so rapidly during this period—her population almost tripled in the 1790s—that it was physically impossible for the churches to keep pace. Most of these newcomers came for land, not for religious reasons, and were more intent on improving their fortunes than their spiritual lives. In the earliest years there simply were no churches for people to attend, and in the absence of churches it was easy for spokesmen to fear that religion was threatened with extinction. To make matters worse, there was bitter intradenominational feuding that discredited religion. The Regular and Separate Baptists disagreed over the acceptance of the Calvinistic Philadelphia Confession of Faith, the morality of slavery, and two ancient church rites: the laying on of hands after baptism and foot washing. The Presbyterians were divided over the use of Isaac Watts's hymns after a straight-laced fanatic, the Reverend Adam Rankin, attacked singing anything but the Psalms of David. Rankin was eventually dismissed from the presbytery, but he persisted in his crusade and successfully gathered about him a small group of tenacious followers. The Methodists were sent reeling from a blow struck at Asbury's control. James O'Kelly fought Asbury's authority to assign circuits and in 1792 split from the Methodists to organize what was called the Republican Methodist church, soon numbering several thousand adherents throughout the South. Such religious disputes brought all religion into disrepute and together with the materialism of the age caused the devout remnant to fear for the future of the faith.

The number of churchgoers probably grew slightly in the 1790s, with only the Methodists suffering an actual decline in membership. Yet set in the midst of a region whose population nearly tripled, even stable membership figures represented a drastic religious decline in terms of influence. This was a regionwide phenomenon, and throughout the South the remaining church folk and their worried clergy desperately sought an answer to what they called a woeful "declension," a loss of "vital piety."

It should cause no surprise that in a period of religious depression there were many who interpreted reality religiously. To say that many Southerners were religious is to describe their general disposition to believe in a God who somehow controls everything. It is not to say they all were intensely pious saints. Likewise the religious decline was simply a perceived slackness in church attendance, a tendency to let religious concerns be overridden by secular ones. In other words, even in the "irreligious"

1790s many if not most southern people were familiar with a certain core of religious beliefs. When confronted with a baffling social phenomenon, an apparent decline in religion that seemed to presage the death of faith, they as all peoples do sought a meaningful explanation of how such a bewildering set of circumstances could have arisen. Not unexpectedly the clergy led in this quest for interpretation, and their congregations followed their path-breaking explication.

The uneasy religious leaders sought an explanation for the current decline in religion within the context of their understanding of how God worked his will on earth. And their explanation proved to be convincing not only because it seemed to fit the situation, but more importantly because it was grounded in the Bible and the popular comprehension of God. They held God to be the supreme Creator, he who made the universe and moment-by-moment oversaw its operation. No detail was too small to catch his notice. Everything that happened, either good or apparently bad, must come under his purview; nothing could occur contrary to his will. A decline in religious interest must, therefore, somehow be related to God's intentions. Even in the midst of their despair ministers intuitively felt that God in the mystery of his ways would shape his purpose out of their dilemma.

Since God controlled everything, and all eventually worked out his purpose, then some good must result from the religious decline. Clearly the outcome must be a purified church, one from which hypocrites and casual members were purged and true believers were forged into better Christians. But why would such drastic divine measures be necessary? God would not act capriciously, would not punish without cause. By sending a period of irreligion and church decline, they reasoned, God was teaching several important lessons, primarily the hurtful effects of living estranged from him. By removing religious prosperity, God showed that it was upon his pleasure that church life and indeed every aspect of life depended. Worldliness, sin, frustration were the fruits of trusting man's power instead of God's. So to save an erring people from this fallacy, God had sent the calamitous times. As a loving parent will force an ill child to swallow distasteful medicine for his own good, so God uses hardship to make better Christians. Out of disappointment and pain, concluded worried Christians as they discovered hope in the final years of the 1790s, would come patience, strength, and fulfillment. Because God had sent an era of decline to teach specific lessons, once Christians showed they had learned the intended lessons, God could confidently be expected to shower them with a renewal of religious zeal.

The fast was the time-tested way of symbolizing the forsaking of worldliness. Consequently throughout the South and in Kentucky, ministers began to call for fasting as a form of public confession. Prayer then was needed for calling upon God for forgiveness and for spiritual aid. And when one earnestly prayed for forgiveness and called for a spiritual refreshing, one could trust God's acceptance and sending of spiritual renewal because God always answered serious, heartfelt prayer. Paradoxically their theology enabled them to find meaning and hope in a situation that originally offered only bewilderment and despair.

Armed with this kind of theological reasoning, clergy across the entire South began urging their congregations to form fast and prayer societies. As a result, the ministers and their flock transformed their decade of despair into a season of hope. As the 1790s came to a close, religious eyes and hearts eagerly awaited a momentous revival, one that no doubt would be marked by miraculous signs that God was surely at work. A spectacular revival that began in Kentucky—the famous Great Revival—was the catalytic event that many of the faithful instantly assumed to be God's action, and throughout the region news of the Kentucky awakening sparked imitation. Cultural and social conditions had led many to crave the feeling of security and community that heartfelt religion offered; consequently a virtual epidemic of revivalism spread almost as if by spontaneous combustion.

There were many factors behind the outbreak of religious fervor in Logan County, Kentucky, in 1800. The climate of expectation was crucial, but other forces were at work. The onrush of migration to Kentucky had outpaced the growth of church organization, and many of the newcomers who had previously been church members desired once more to become affiliated with a community of believers. In a rapidly changing and mobile society, people yearned for the sense of belonging provided by church membership. Moreover, strict church discipline had resulted in many backsliders being excommunicated, and often they desired reinstatement. Most of Kentucky and the South were peopled not by educated gentry but by the poorer sort for whom the emotional ecstasy provided by the evangelical churches was comforting and meaningful. Religious revivals also draw a disproportionate amount of converts from youths, and the backcountry South, especially southern Kentucky and Tennessee, had a high percentage of its population under age fourteen. These social and cultural forces, existing in an atmosphere of heady expectation, produced a Kentucky primed for a veritable religious explosion. The spark that ignited the region into general conflagration was the entry into Kentucky of an experienced and dramatic evangelist, the Reverend James McGready.

McGready was born about 1760 in western Pennsylvania, but in 1778 his Scotch-Irish Presbyterian parents moved the family to North Carolina. Several years later McGready returned to Pennsylvania to study with two respected Presbyterian evangelicals, Joseph Smith and John McMillan. Under their tutelage McGready became a scintillating orator, and, after being licensed to preach in 1788, he set out for his home in the North Carolina Piedmont. On his way through Virginia he chanced to visit Hampden-Sydney College which at that time was in the midst of a memorable student religious revival. Combined with his earlier training, this on-the-scene encounter convinced McGready that hard-hitting revival sermons were the key to winning souls. Once he had established himself in Guilford County, North Carolina, McGready launched an intensive revival campaign, invading the easy conscience of the dominant planters as well as the more willing hearts of the yeomen. Soon with the latter he gained great triumphs, including several who later became Presbyterian ministers in Kentucky, but with the former he met stiff opposition. McGready persisted, bombarding the better classes with charges of hypocrisy, materialism, and sin. His commanding size, piercing eyes, penetrating voice, and guilt-provoking words made him impossible to ignore, and his opponents threatened him with death if he did not cease his supplications. Blood smeared on his pulpit convinced McGready that his life was in danger. Seizing the opportunity provided when former parishioners now in Kentucky sent him a call, he resigned his North Carolina ministry for more peaceful fields west of the Appalachians. In late 1796 McGready arrived in Logan County, Kentucky, which Peter Cartwright described as a "rogue's harbor."

The following January, McGready took charge of three small churches—Red River, Muddy River, and Gasper River—in Logan County, and though he preached with his usual zeal, he was ineffective. During the bleak winter of 1797–1798 he was able to get his sparse congregations "to observe the third Saturday of each month, for one year, as a day of fasting and prayer, for the conversion of sinners in Logan County, and throughout the world." In addition they promised to spend a half hour on Saturday evenings and Sunday mornings "in pleading with God to revive his work." For the next two years McGready tirelessly preached and prayed with steady but not spectacular results. A service in July 1799 at the Red River Church saw a religious zeal new to

Logan County, and at a similar meeting a month later at Gasper River, a small revival developed so suddenly even McGready was surprised. Dozens of churchgoers literally fell deathlike to the floor overcome with their convictions of sin and their belief that the wages of sin was death.

The unusual physical phenomena and conspicuous conversions were soon the talk of the countryside, and the foothills must have buzzed as people looked forward to McGready's next meeting. Interest leaped; curiosity seekers could hardly wait; devout churchgoers wondered if this was the beginning of their long awaited deliverance. At each successive meeting the crowds grew larger, the religious services more animated, the results more striking. The winter cold postponed the ever-larger meetings that were already overflowing the small churches, and McGready spent the winter months hoping that the current slack was but the proverbial calm before a revival whirlwind.

The first truly extraordinary demonstration of religious fervor came in June 1800. That month several hundred of the most devout members of McGready's three churches gathered at the Red River meetinghouse for a communion service; McGready was assisted by two colleagues, the Reverends William Hodge and John Rankin. The first three days of the four-day affair were completely normal, but Monday was different. Two new ministers, the brothers John and William McGee, on their way to Ohio had stopped at the services, and, because William had been a convert of McGready in North Carolina, the two were asked to join the preaching even though John was a Methodist. William Hodge preached on Sunday, and suddenly in the middle of his sermon a woman began shouting and singing, then stopped as suddenly as she had begun. Hodge concluded his sermon, and he, McGready, and Rankin prepared to leave the church. The two McGee brothers stayed on, and so did the congregation.

William, filled with excitement, stood up to speak but was overcome with emotion and sat on the floor, weeping. The congregation, now on edge and beginning to sob, waited, not knowing what to expect next. John, the Methodist who had experience in stoking the fires of religious zeal and emotion, rose and with tremulous fervor began to exhort the crowd, telling them that the Holy Spirit was present. The congregation, their nerves tingling at this suggestion that God in his miracle-working power was in their midst, broke out into cries and shouts. McGready, Hodge, and Rankin stood by aghast, but decided to let McGee continue his preaching. McGee in turn went down the aisle shouting, exhorting with great loudness and excitement, and immediately the congregation caught his religious fever, falling to the floor in a state of semiconsciousness. When the services ended the ministers concluded they had just witnessed a miraculous visitation of the Holy Spirit.

News spread rapidly of this extraordinary event, and McGready quickly capitalized on its notoriety by scheduling another sacramental service at the Gasper River Church. He made elaborate preparations, sending the news far and wide. Knowing curiosity and the expectation that God at any time might begin his work of revival would attract large crowds, McGready advised churchgoers and ministers to come prepared to stay the duration of the meeting. McGready's advertising was unnecessary, for as rumors of the Red River revival raced across Logan County, eager crowds prepared to attend the Gasper River meeting.

The services began on Friday of the last weekend of July 1800. By early morning unprecedented crowds had begun to gather, many prepared to remain for as long as the services continued. This was to be the first "camp meeting," later a southern institution. The huge numbers in attendance, their interdenominational nature, and the general air of anticipation infused the scene with a kind of intuitive awareness that this was to be a special occasion.

On Saturday night the cumulation of two days of preaching bore fruit: two women began shouting. Soon the floor was covered with motionless penitents, convicted of sin and praying for forgiveness. The ministers worked through the night and into Sunday morning. Conversion became almost a social contagion as peer pressure, exhaustion, and near hysterical excitement overcame many persons' hesitation. Spectacular actions symbolic of conviction and conversion temporarily became the cultural norm. Impressionable young children particularly were caught up by the revival and converted in great numbers. The whole aura of the meeting, with its huge crowds, frenetic preaching by a variety of ministers for hour upon hour, the tents and wagons strewn across the churchyard, the torches casting their flickering shadows, the moans of conviction and joyous shouts of comforting conversion, gave the Gasper River revival an image of soul-stirring novelty. Nothing like this had ever been seen before, and occurring in the context of a decade of religious decline that had been transformed into hope, the Gasper River happening was widely interpreted as heralding what had so long been anticipated. Because of this image which it gained instantly, Gasper River became the catalytic agent that set off a chain reaction of similar revivals, sweeping first across Kentucky and then across the entire South.

The revival seemed to spread with accounts of its previous outbreaks, multiplying in its march through the state. Its greatest manifestation came in Bourbon County in August 1801 at a small church called Cane Ridge. This gigantic meeting came to be the archetype of the Great Revival camp meetings, its fame spreading far and wide. Barton W. Stone was the Presbyterian minister at Cane Ridge, but he had found apathy there since his arrival in 1798. Then he began to hear of the wonderful work in Logan County being directed by James McGready, whom Stone had known in North Carolina. Stone decided in the early summer of 1801 to travel to Logan County to examine for himself the revival. When he arrived he saw that here was no ordinary religious awakening. "The scene to me was new," he wrote, "and passing strange. It baffled description." Convinced he had witnessed the work of God, Stone returned to Cane Ridge, determined to evoke a successful revival there. This proved to be an easy task, for the cultural and social conditions in Bourbon County were similar to those in Logan County. Immediately he began to make preparations for a mighty revival to be held in early August 1801 at Cane Ridge.

The small log meetinghouse at Cane Ridge was on the slope of a large, gently inclined hill, with shade trees to offer protection from the blazing August sun and a refreshing stream nearby. The advance publicity had its effect, for early on Friday, August 8, the roads and trails converging on Cane Ridge were filled with horses, wagons, and walkers. This was near the heavily populated center of the state, and the crowd eventually was numbered between twelve and twenty-five thousand. Even allowing for ministerial exaggeration, this was a phenomenal crowd.

Thousands of worshipers were scattered across the hillside. Sermons, hymns, hosannas, weeping filled the air. Ministers, perched atop stumps, standing among the limbs of half-fallen trees, or astride wagons, warned at the top of their voices of the judgment day to come and the opportunity now for salvation. Eighteen Presbyterian ministers were present, and possibly more Baptist and Methodist. There were clumps of listeners around various speakers and here and there a flurry of excitement as someone fell to the ground "convicted of sin" or as some new convert, man or woman, adult or child, began to give expression to present joy. The thousands in attendance, mingling their voices and excitement with others, the wagons and tents encircling the grounds, the never-ending sermons and religious services that produced the exhaustion and near prostration, the clamor and confusion of such numbers—to hundreds of participants, God seemed quite evidently to be at hand. One does not have to be versed in crowd psychology to recognize the impact of such remarkable revival scenes on the participants whose "powers of contemplation" were "swallowed up" by the surrounding events.

Cane Ridge was also the setting for the first occurrence of those bizarre physical "exercises" which to the popular mind today characterized the Great Revival. The psychological and social origins of these phenomena are still unknown. Perhaps those undergoing them were so desperately seeking some sign of assurance of their salvation that they unconsciously generated the extravagant responses as vivid proof of the genuineness of their conversion. Some recent research suggests there is little difference between what is called "hypnotism" and a "high level of suggestibility." In a situation where such exercises were assumed to be the work of the Holy Spirit, perhaps a kind of social hypnosis or intense social suggestibility provided by peer pressure resulted in the famous revival exercises.

There were seven categories of revival responses: the falling exercise, the rolling exercise, the "jerks," the barking exercise, the dancing exercise, and the laughing and singing exercises. As their names suggest, the latter three revival symptoms were uncontrollable singing, laughing, and dancing performed in joyful ecstasy. The falling exercise was the collapsing on the floor or ground in a semiconscious catatonic state. Many persons after a while arose to give exultant testimony of having "met Jesus." According to later accounts the rolling exercise consisted of fervent believers falling and rolling around like logs. Extravagant tales have been told of participants rolling through mud and even on occasion grasping their ankles with their hands and rolling hooplike. The widely reported jerking was undoubtedly a genuine revival response. Many accounts tell of listeners suddenly beginning a fast and spasmodic jerking of their body and limbs. The so-called barks were probably an exaggeration of the natural grunts elicited by the more familiar jerks. Wild stories have circulated of demented Christians barking up trees—"treeing the Devil"—and of churchgoers running through the woods like a pack of dogs, but both these stories were certainly invented to discredit the revival.

In spite of the extravagant publicity given by later historians, the more extreme revival exercises were probably restricted to a comparative few except in the very early years of the revival. Critics of evangelical, emotional revivalism used farfetched stories of revival extremes to bring the whole movement into disrepute. Revival supporters were often driven to support exercises they otherwise would have frowned upon because of their opponents, and they defended the unusual phenomena as sent by God as a signal of his Spirit working in truly unusual ways to renew "vital piety." At most camp meetings shouting, crying, and falling down were the only accepted physical responses to impassioned preaching. For a people abruptly and intensely aware of their spiritual shortcomings, these were recognizably symbolic means of articulating their changed state of existence. They were physical ways of expressing fears and joys most revival participants were too uneducated and too momentarily involved to communicate in more conventional terms. And in a cultural situation demanding emphatic revelation of one's spiritual status, these exercises became a sort of shorthand to revival participants.

In the aftermath of Cane Ridge and its lesser successors, religion for a time came to monopolize the popular mind in Kentucky. One traveler to Lexington in October 1802 heard "of but little else than the great revival of religion." So prevalent were the tales of casual passersby falling stricken with sin at the camp meetings that this traveler actually "felt much anxiety lest [he] should fall down when amongst them." Later that year a correspondent from Frankfort wrote: "It is a very comfortable thing to be in a country where religion has obtained the pre-eminent influence. That is those that have it show it, and those that have it not wish to be considered religious for the credit it gives in the society." Such literary evidence of the revival impact is corroborated by the actual statistics of church growth. Between 1800 and 1802 the six Baptist associations in Kentucky grew in membership from 4,766 to 13,569. In the five years following the beginning of the camp meetings, the Western Conference of the Methodist church, consisting of the districts of Tennessee and Kentucky, expanded from 3,030 members to 10,158. Churches were organized, religious communities created, a sense of Christian order was formed out of the chaos of frontier mobility. The Presbyterians prospered but slightly, having most of their revival converts siphoned off by two schisms that developed out of their denomination: the Christians (Disciples of Christ) and the Cumberland Presbyterians. The rapid expansion of the churches formed the basis of Francis Asbury's 1806 remark about Kentucky which, he stated, "was a few years [ago] a dangerous frontier, . . . [but now is] the centre of the western front of our [Christian] empire."

The camp-meeting revival was more than a technique of simply enlarging church roles; it became a ritual whereby the participants' religious comprehension—that God had sent the purifying declension and was now providing deliverance—was given ceremonial authenticity. The revival confirmed the people's religious interpretation of reality. Throughout Kentucky and the South thousands whose religious beliefs had been only nominal, almost subliminal, found their faith invigorated by the revival. The revival in the beginning served to awaken latent beliefs and recruit thousands into active church membership. In subsequent years revivals became a recurring ritual by means of which evangelical Protestantism was periodically energized to such an extent that it became a major force in southern society.

Consequently the Great Revival altered the course of

Kentucky and southern history. As a result of its stimulus to laymen and clergy, evangelical Protestantism, especially in its Baptist and Methodist varieties, was placed on such a foundation that never again was Protestant dominance threatened in the South. More liberal Protestant movements never really had a chance in the region after the plain folk had tasted the emotional fulfillment of pietistic revivalism in which individuals were pressured to seize their salvation. The Roman Catholic church was to make a distinguished record in the Bluegrass State, but it never came close to challenging the strength of the Baptists, Methodists, and Presbyterians. And a peculiar cast of mind—highly individualistic, localistic, and conversion-oriented—was laid over the southern populace by the forces emanating from the Great Revival. Rich and poor, genteel and "clod-hoppers," planters and plain folk, black and white came to share this revivalistic frame of reference. A genuine folk culture emerged, one that exalted the individual and the identification with locale. Much that is associated with the southern character may be linked to conservative religion, and the Great Revival, beginning in Kentucky and spreading into the remainder of the South, was largely responsible for that relationship. Yet the unity of southern thought was not complete—there were divisions and schisms—and paradoxically the Great Revival also contributed to the religious diversity of the Bluegrass State.

3

RELIGIOUS DIVERSITY

THE GREAT REVIVAL at the beginning of the nineteenth century had repercussions that affected many aspects of Kentucky culture. Evangelical religion emerged from the revival maelstrom so invigorated that from that time on it characterized Kentucky Protestantism. It was an individualistic and otherworldly faith that ministered to the expectations and frustrations of the average people. Despite the prevailing myth of easy social mobility, thousands lived only slightly above the subsistence level. These were not the wealthy nabobs of plantation legend, but rather the majority who filled the church pews, worked their few acres, and lived and died in obscurity. A religion that placed higher values on salvation and piety than on one's worldly estate surely met the needs of most Kentuckians.

This religion taught that the most important thing in the world was living a life of faith in order to inherit eternal life in heaven. Those who felt assured of this inheritance found failure in worldly things ultimately unimportant. By providing the camp meeting and the conversion experience—often annually updated through "rededication"—evangelical religion offered a ritualistic escape from the burden of sin, and this was an important function in a slaveholding society. Because it presented Jesus as the one who died for all alike, regardless of their station in life, it was a democratic faith that was profoundly comforting to most Kentuckians. Through their faith people could find meaning and value in life and hence gain a degree of self-respect that allowed a southern folk culture to develop. Southern religion powerfully mitigated against any incipient class feelings that otherwise might have erupted between the poorer whites and the planters. As the evangelical denominations grew in size, affluence, and prestige, they gained immense influence in Kentucky. By mid-century persons in all levels of society generally accepted the views of evangelical religion. Kentucky and the South were solid religiously before they became solid politically.

The emotional and social needs of the plain folk called forth in the Great Revival a particular religious response, and the precise shape of that response exerted a homogenizing influence on all religions. The Methodists and Baptists were closely related to the people to begin with and easily adjusted their techniques and beliefs to fit the revival mode which they perfected. But Presbyterians had a more rigid theology and stringent rules, and the popular forces emanating from the Great Revival brought pressures for adaptation that the Presbyterian structure could not stand. The result was a series of ruptures that paved the way for the Shakers to enter the West and that left schisms producing two new denominations, the Cumberland Presbyterians and the Disciples of Christ. Paradoxically the Great Revival, which promised religious harmony, not only begat an evangelical culture that came to characterize the southern mind but also brought forth stresses that cracked existing church structures. A greater degree of religious diversity was the long-range heritage of the Great Revival.

Richard McNemar and Barton W. Stone were two Presbyterian ministers who began to experiment with the evangelical ideas that were prevalent in the early years of the nineteenth century, and the logic of their beliefs, combined with repressive denominational opposition, led them into new systems of faith. Stone, the promoter of the Cane Ridge camp meeting, had been born in Maryland and converted under the preaching of James McGready in North Carolina. During his ordination examination Stone said that he accepted the Westminster Confession of Faith only so far as he "saw it consistent with the word of God." Since none of the examining ministers objected, the independent-minded Stone was ordained. Years later when he came to differ with Presbyterian authorities, he fell back on his reading of the Scriptures as the bedrock of his faith and developed what eventually became a separate denomination. McNemar was a singularly attractive, talented, and influential minister who also had a mind of his own: at the end of the 1790s, for example, he eagerly anticipated the imminent Second Coming of Christ. When, in the course of the Great Revival, he began to shift to the left theologically, he had a significant impact ultimately on the supreme heresy in the West: the Shaker religion.

At the Cane Ridge camp meeting McNemar and Stone were remarkably fervent even for the occasion; indeed, so unusual were the sentiments they expressed that a more conservative Presbyterian colleague, John Lyle, confided to his diary his apprehensions that the two were preaching unorthodox theology. McNemar and Stone had previously broached a willingness to assume they were privy to spiritual truth, and now that the Cane Ridge extravaganza seemed to be upsetting the applecart of Calvinist orthodoxy, they were emboldened to tell the shocked Lyle they were preaching the true new gospel possessed only by them. Rejecting the more limited view that salvation was engendered in a relative few solely because of the working of God's mysterious Spirit, McNemar and Stone argued that the gospel news itself, when understood and accepted, brought pardon and regeneration. Today this might seem like a trivial issue, but in 1801 such a view represented a major deviation from the understanding of the central role of the Holy Spirit shared by all the evangelical groups. The Methodists and Baptists held that the Spirit was generously infused into the hearts of sinners, but they with the Presbyterians accepted the idea of grace. Had McNemar and Stone been members of these other two denominations that were less rigorous theologically, perhaps their nonconforming views would have been ignored in the midst of the revival tumult. But since they were Presbyterians, the local presbytery got wind of shifting views and quickly called the offenders to task.

Gaining momentum with their extreme evangelical views, McNemar (often preaching across the river in the Ohio Territory) and Stone (stationed in north central Kentucky) quickly attracted crowds of eager supporters. And just as promptly the theologically fastidious Washington Presbytery brought charges against McNemar, about whom rumors had reached certain stern ears. Before a meeting of the presbytery McNemar was accused of preaching "dangerous and pernicious" ideas and, among other things, of embracing Arminian principles. No one came forward to substantiate the charges, McNemar resolutely said he was bound to nothing but the Holy Scriptures, and for the present time the presbytery had to settle for an admonition. Yet those whom Stone called "sticklers for orthodoxy" were not satisfied. Possibly recognizing that there was a tendency for others caught up in the revival to depart from the strict confines of doctrine, the Washington Presbytery decided to make of McNemar a lesson for potential deviates.

Consequently on October 6, 1802, the presbytery met again, and an elder this time did complain personally of McNemar's false teachings. After a close examination the presbytery decided the accused was in fact teaching new doctrines, although they "were clothed in such expression" as to camouflage the errors from all but the most discerning. Even though the presbytery concluded that McNemar's views were "dangerous to the souls of man, and hostile to the interests of all true religion," they permitted him to continue preaching at the six churches he served. Perhaps they hoped their verbal chastisement would persuade McNemar to abandon his views; perhaps they also feared an outright prohibition of his preaching would make him a martyr and thus gain for him additional support. More probably the presbytery simply hesitated to rule controversially against so popular a preacher and chose instead to hand the case on to the Synod of Kentucky.

Convening in Lexington on September 6, 1803, the synod received the case of Richard McNemar. Again charges were brought and witnesses heard; the synod by a vote of seventeen to six (with one abstention) upheld the presbytery's charges against McNemar and even reproved it for allowing him to continue preaching. The synod vote followed a theological cleavage that was rapidly developing in the state. The six votes for McNemar were all by ministers leaning toward theological revision. The battle lines were drawn between the revisionists and the conservatives. The followers of Stone and McNemar recognized that henceforth no deviation from safe doctrine would be allowed. As Stone wrote, the synod's action "not only involved the fate of McNemar . . . , but equally our own. We saw the arm of ecclesiastical authority raised to crush us, and we must either sink, or step aside to avoid the blow." While the synod was in a short recess, five of the dissenters (including McNemar and Stone) met together and agreed to protest the synod's action, to declare their independence of the synod, and thus be freed from confining supervision.

When the Synod of Kentucky was notified of the rebels' decision, it sent a committee to try to argue them out of their position. This attempt failed (one member from the committee even joined the dissenters), so the synod promptly suspended them and declared their churches vacant. The dissenters, now seeing that the break was irreconcilable, accepted independence and to signify their position constituted themselves in late 1803 as a new entity under the name of the Springfield Presbytery. In response to the request of the synod, they published a lengthy pamphlet, *An Apology for Renouncing the Jurisdiction of the Synod of Kentucky* (January 1804), which outlined their view of the events culminating in this secession and the theology they professed. The section of the *Apology* entitled "Compendious View of the Gospel" revealed that Stone and the others had in fact moved far beyond orthodox Calvinism. Denying that fallen man was totally deprived of rational faculties, totally unable as a sinner to have faith without the intervening power of God's grace, the dissenters argued that man by his reason could hear and respond to the gospel. Faith was generated by reasonable persons accepting the testimony of the gospel, and as such, faith was available to all who would so listen and consider scripture, not restricted to some arbitrary elect.

Probably few of the popular supporters of Stone and McNemar were concerned with theological precision and careful definition. The reformers were charismatic preachers with an appealing and democratic doctrine, and that was sufficient to attract a following. But if the orthodox were upset by the *Apology*, they had only to wait a short while before being shocked even further. McNemar, who by this time was emerging as the leader of the schismatics, had proceeded one step further from the Presbyterian Confession. He decided that even the independent Springfield Presbytery was a division of the organized denomination and as such impeded the work of God. McNemar composed a document that proclaimed the dissolution of the Springfield Presbytery. The dissenter movement, whose members were now called New Lights, was moving rapidly into a new phase.

Freed from the limitations of a Confession of Faith, the schismatics were at liberty both to experiment with their own ideas and to be persuaded by those of others. At this fortuitous juncture the Reverend Rice Haggard came into contact with the impressionable McNemar. For ten years, beginning in Virginia, Haggard had been urging that all Christians should unite, eschew all denominational identity, and call themselves simply "Christians." Moved by a vision of Christian union and harmony if all sectarian labels and differences were dismissed, creeds forgotten, and scripture alone used for the basis of belief, McNemar threw all his support behind the "Christian" movement. The dissenters were swayed to drop their party label, "Springfield Presbytery." As a result they issued a pamphlet authored by Haggard, *An Address to the Different Religious Societies on the Sacred Import of the Christian Name,* and McNemar announced the death of their organization in a curious document called "The Last Will and Testament of the Springfield Presbytery." They pledged themselves to work for the cause of Christian unity with the Bible as a common creed.

Despite the advocacy of a Christian unity that submerged all differences, the six dissenters who signed the "Last Will and Testament" were not together long. McNemar and Stone were obviously the leaders, and, as they went different directions, the New Lights split apart. McNemar, the more radical of the two, had long entertained millennial expectations. Hoping the end times were near, he eagerly looked for signs that presaged the Second Coming. With this outlook, and his demonstrated willingness to sample new ideas, McNemar was an easy touch for the most heretical missionaries in all America, Mother Ann Lee's followers, whom the world knew as Shakers. The United Society of Believers in Christ's Second Appearance, as they called themselves, believed that the millennium had already begun, since Jesus had returned in the female form of Ann Lee, completing the incarnation. Having emigrated from England to New York in 1774 and growing steadily, the Shakers had long awaited an opportunity to move west. Mother Lee herself had even spoken prophetically of "the opening of the gospel in the western country." Because in New York the

Shakers had gained most of their recruits in the aftermath of evangelical revivals, they expected a similar harvest from the Kentucky revivals. The New York community therefore sent three missionaries on a "pedistrial [*sic*] journey of more than a thousand miles . . . . to visit the subjects of the revival, in that country, with a view to search out the state of their minds, and open the testimony of salvation to them." In early spring 1805 the Shaker emissaries arrived and began to spread their message in northern Kentucky.

The Shakers could not have chosen a more fruitful time to begin their western mission. The New Lights, exuberant in their new theological freedom and zealous for perfection and complete assurance of their salvation, were ripe to be plucked by the Shakers trained in garnering revival enthusiasts. Barton W. Stone later remembered the Shakers as neatly but plainly dressed, unpretentious in their manner, enormously learned in the Scriptures, and "of great boldness in their faith." They offered the New Lights the enticing promise of total fulfillment in gospel love and perfection. The very first person to whom the Shaker missionaries spoke, Malcolm Worley, was a fervent New Light, and he promptly accepted the Shaker vision. Almost as quickly McNemar and two other New Light leaders, Matthew Houston and John Dunlavy, were converts to the novel testimony which offered "actual possession of . . . salvation."

Stone was deeply shaken by this turn of events, for he saw that the road from doctrinal standards seemed to be leading to theological anarchism and religious irresponsibility. Rather than increasing Christian unity the New Lights were splintering into a Babel of confused voices. Determined to salvage the mission for Christian unity if at all possible, Stone began a concerted plan to contain the spread of Shakerism and stop its impressment of revival converts. "Never," he wrote, "did I exert myself more than at this time to save the people from this vortex of ruin." The New Light movement had thus come to a fork in the road. McNemar and the more extreme proponents of millennialism took the radical route, while Stone emerged as the leader of those who chose the path they hoped would lead to Christian unity. In a way the Shaker inroad proved to be a godsend for Stone, for it removed the more fanatic element from the "Christian" party and allowed it to delineate its theology. Even though two of the original New Lights, Robert Marshall and John Thompson, withdrew from the Stoneite movement and reunited with the Presbyterians, the Stoneites continued until they merged with another similar movement begun by Alexander Campbell, and the result was the Disciples of Christ.

David Purviance, who with Stone fought the Shaker advance, came to realize the unforeseen benefits of the winnowing. "I have thought," he later wrote, "there might be something providential in the coming of the Shakers, although some honest and precious souls were seduced and ruined by their means; yet a growing fanaticism was drawn out of the church, which threatened the most deleterious effects." This "growing fanaticism," however, had a history of its own that left striking physical remains in Kentucky: the Shaker communities of Pleasant Hill in Mercer County and South Union in Logan County.

The Shaker missionaries had the quiet and confident zeal of those who believe with certainty that they possess the ultimate truth, and shunning the tumult of camp meetings where the more orthodox ministers attacked them, they stealthily conversed with individuals. So successful were their efforts that the original three were soon joined by additional missionaries from New York. The greatest obstacle to Shaker conversion was its requirement of celibacy, which some critics charged was but a ploy to divide families and steal their property. Partly to put this criticism to rest, but primarily because it was consistent with their communal emphasis, groups of Shakers who were already living in communistic fashion in private homes began to pool their resources to purchase sites for their own communities. In 1806 at both South Union and Pleasant Hill the first acquisition of land began. Soon stone houses, barns, and other improvements were added. At each location groups of believers called families lived in large, dormitorylike houses. The sexes were rigidly segregated, and the society was organized along functional lines. All the members were gainfully employed in the multitude of chores; each worked to support the community. There was no private ownership of property and as little social commerce with the outside world as possible. A genuine feeling of shared community made the Shaker villages a wholesome anomaly in the individualistic society of early Kentucky.

Because of their devotion to hard work and simple living, the Shaker communities became marvels of agricultural efficiency. Completely self-sufficient, they built sawmills, gristmills, cider mills, tanneries, distilleries, blacksmith shops, wheelwright shops, shoemaker's shops, lime and brick kilns; made cheese, bonnets, and straw hats for sale; opened a tavern for visitors; operated a post office; sold livestock and fruits to surrounding neighbors; and perfected the preparation and packaging of seeds for sale. The South Union village each year sent a boat to New Orleans filled with their widely sought seeds, dried fruits, and small implements. The Shakers were known for their handy tools which combined simplicity of design with utility. In a sense these mechanical devices symbolized the sparsely functional design of Shaker buildings, furniture, even their communal social relations. No unnecessary actions, no dysfunctional bric-a-brac intruded upon their lives or their architectural designs. So successful were these spiritual communes, these millenarian monasteries, that they sparked a widespread American interest in communitarian experiments during the first half of the nineteenth century. Reaching a top membership in Kentucky of perhaps 800 or 900 (approximately 6,000 nationally), the Shaker communities in Kentucky slowly declined after the 1850s until they went out of existence in the early twentieth century.

The Shaker beliefs were as novel in 1810 as they are today, and, combined with the seancelike spiritualism of their efforts to communicate with the dead, they made an exotic addition to religious life in early Kentucky. All visitors were intrigued by the ritualistic singing and dancing of the Shaker religious services. At first the dancing, jerking, shouting, and singing were only more flagrant examples of the previously mentioned revival exercises; after all, most Shaker converts were revival enthusiasts who sought experiences beyond those offered by traditional Protestantism. Gradually these activities calmed down, became stylized, and soon the ring dance became the trademark of Shakerism. The so-called warring gift consisted of sweeping motions with the arms and hands as the worshipers marched around the room to the accompaniment of a lively tune.

While the tourist attraction of such ceremonies is obvious (the Shakers finally had to restrict visitors), the legitimacy of Stone's fear that Shakerism was a wildly heretical disruption of his dreams of Christian unity is equally clear. Carefully feeling his way toward a theological position, Stone found doctrinal disputes over minor issues disheartening. He developed a leniency toward all those who embraced the simple essentials of early Christianity. Although he believed elders and ministers should be set apart from the congregations, he defended congregational autonomy and was opposed to interchurch tribunals such as had dismissed the Springfield six. Moreover, in his opposition to creeds he was hesitant to prescribe doctrinal standards, but, since he also could not accept some aspects of the Westminster Confession, he felt he should outline his own beliefs in the hopes that many would accept them. Thus for the next quarter century as Barton W. Stone steadily preached and built up his

"Christian connexion"—he did not want to create yet another denomination—he also developed a system of thought.

At his ordination Stone had openly admitted that he could accept no creedal statement he found in contradiction to his own reading of the Bible, and early in the Great Revival he had questioned the role of grace in initiating conversion. It comes as no surprise to learn that Stone's mature theology dealt with such issues. While the Scriptures remained the basis of his faith, it was a faith erected on a rational analysis of the Bible. In his literalism and rationalism Stone combined two powerful influences in early religion. He simply could not accept the prevailing theories of atonement. Considering the idea of substitutionary atonement both unscriptural and irrational, he believed that Christ was sent to reconcile men to God, not to change God's mind. Even sinners possessed enough reason to understand the New Testament story and from that testimony come to accept God without the need of a miraculous intrusion of grace. A similar approach led Stone to break with traditional Trinitarianism. He argued that the Holy Spirit was God working, not a separate person in the Trinity. In like fashion he considered Christ a separate person, God's son, and not coequal or coexistent with God. The Scriptures, he believed, do not elaborate a Trinitarian doctrine, and reason does not support such a view, so Stone dissented from still another orthodox dogma. In a series of pamphlets and articles Stone made his views widely known in Kentucky and the Midwest. By 1827 his followers numbered 3,350 in Kentucky and almost 13,000 in all.

Another ingredient was yet to be added to the Kentucky-led movement, and that was to be provided by the father-son combination of Thomas and Alexander Campbell. Thomas Campbell (1763–1854) was a Scotch-Irish minister in the Seceder Presbyterian Church who in search of a better opportunity to work for Christian unity emigrated to Pennsylvania in 1807. Stationed in southwestern Pennsylvania, within three months he was at odds with the synod over his desire that all churches be united in a return to primitive Christianity. Soon he withdrew from the synod and began preaching in homes near Washington, Pennsylvania. By 1809 he had organized the "Christian Association of Washington" which in its complete literalism accepted Campbell's dictum, "Where the Scriptures speak, we speak; where the Scriptures are silent, we are silent." At first Campbell professed no intention to organize a new denomination, but almost immediately he was pointing out doctrinal errors in surrounding churches. In his *Declaration and Address of the Christian Association of Washington* (1809) he presented his plans to secure Christian unity on his own terms which he based solely upon his interpretation of the New Testament. Beliefs contrary to those he accepted were implicitly contrary to the teachings of the New Testament.

Of signal importance to Campbell's program was the return in late 1809 from a year at the University of Glasgow of his son Alexander. The younger Campbell (1788–1866) was bright, argumentative, aggressive, and a good promoter. Accepting his father's views—in fact he had independently arrived at similar conclusions—he was to become a truly significant figure in American religious history, combining with even greater acumen than Stone the principles of rationalism with a return to scriptural literalism and primitive Christianity. But for the first few years the Campbells experienced bleak prospects, their movement seemingly at a stalemate. They sought to reform and unite the denominations, not create another church. However, failure forced them to concede to reality, and the Christian Association reconstituted itself an independent entity, the Brush Run Church, in the spring of 1811. Since the Campbells saw total immersion as the biblically enjoined form of baptism, they in 1813 sought and were granted admission to the Redstone Baptist Association. The Campbell group did not surrender any principles, for they joined with the reservation that "we should be allowed to teach and preach whatever we learn from the Holy Scriptures, regardless of any human creed or formula in Christendom."

For the next fifteen years the Campbells remained nominally Baptists, with Alexander even editing (1823–1829) an influential periodical entitled the *Christian Baptist*. But the followers of the Campbells, considering themselves Christian Reformers and called by others "Campbellites," were never really Baptists. Though they did advocate baptism by immersion, there the real similarity ended, for as the Campbells developed their theology they effected a genuine departure from the traditional orthodoxy. On the key issue of the nature of baptism, the Baptists believed it to be a symbolic public confession of one's prior conversion; the Reformers held that regeneration followed baptism—in fact, rather than as a symbol. The Reformers argued that as a command of Christ baptism was necessary for the remission of sin. Rejecting the mysterious efficacy of grace, the Campbells insisted that the Scriptures alone spoke to sinners and led them to conversion. Moreover, the Reformers celebrated Communion on each Lord's day, practically ignored the Old Testament in their total preoccupation with the New, and emphatically rejected all forms of ecclesiastical organization above the level of the local congregation. Mission societies, for example, were abhorred as incompatible with the New Testament, since the Scriptures do not mention them. The Reformers were at first very successful in the Baptist camp, drawing thousands attracted by their immersionist principles and then leading them to their more radical new doctrines. Quickly the Baptist leaders recognized what was happening, for the Reformers were in their eyes wolves in Baptist clothing. The result was a long and bitter warfare between the Reformers and Baptists, with the Reformers finally dropping all affiliation with the Baptists about 1830.

By that date the Reformers, now being called "Disciples of Christ" as they moved further away from denominational labels and called for Christian unity under their banner, had gained still another giant, Walter Scott. Scott was a marvelously effective preacher, and with his talents added to the organizational, debating, and promotional abilities of Alexander Campbell, the "Christian Reformers" were preparing for substantial growth. Scott was a Scotsman, a graduate of the University of Edinburgh who after coming to America in 1818 was introduced to the idea of abandoning the then-present bane, competing congregations, and returning to the ideal of primitive Christianity. By the winter of 1821–1822 when he met Alexander Campbell, Scott was well advanced toward a theology that made a virtue of great simplicity. Preaching in Ohio and Kentucky, he devised a simple and dramatic device to teach his views in easily memorable form. Holding up his hand, he would count off his five major points: faith, repentance, baptism, remission of sins, and the gift of the Holy Spirit. This "five finger exercise" proved so popular and effective a summary of the preacher's beliefs that with it Scott made enormous numbers of converts. The plain folk liked its directness, its simplicity, and its rejection of the miraculous. Here was offered an easy, certain, and dependable way to salvation, and thousands in Kentucky and the Midwest accepted it. The Disciples of Christ were becoming a major force with which to reckon.

Barton W. Stone of the "Christian Connexion" and Alexander Campbell of the "Christian Reformers," now called Disciples, had met in 1824 and were instantly aware of their similarities. At the same time they were cognizant of significant differences; in particular Campbell was somewhat leery of Stone's anti-Trinitarianism, and Stone was put off by what he felt was Campbell's tendency to promote himself and his views on the purpose of baptism. Moreover, Stone was much more of a revivalist than was Campbell. Nevertheless they often spoke to the same kinds of people and recognized that in general they were spiritual brothers in the midst of orthodox opposition. As the leaders and their respective congregations came slowly to know each other better, their differences were smoothed over, and in 1832 at a meeting in Lexington a loose merger was effected. In one sense Stone's Christian party was swallowed up by the larger Disciples movement, but the resulting new denomination was to have a significant impact on the religious life of Kentucky and the entire region. It faced unrelenting religious strife instigated especially by the Baptists, who correctly saw the Disciples of Christ as a movement with new—and to the Baptists heretical— ideas which was successfully drawing to itself whole congregations of Baptists. Yet with effective leadership and a doctrine composed of equal parts of rationalism and biblical literalism that proved most attractive in the West, the Disciples of Christ overcame their opposition to become a major denomination. From a total of some 22,000 members in 1832 at the time of the merger, by 1860 according to the best estimates there were approximately 192,000 Disciples of Christ, with 45,000 in Kentucky alone. Such fantastic growth illustrates the effectiveness and also suggests the influence of the indigenous new denomination born in America with strong roots in Kentucky.

The Great Revival, from which excitement came Stone's original break with orthodoxy and the Shaker experiment in the West, also produced another schism that resulted in still another denomination. The example of the immediate past—New Lights, Shakers, and the Disciples movement—greatly influenced the development of the subsequent division. The Stone-McNemar controversy had centered in northern Kentucky and neighboring regions of Ohio, but the Presbyterian church from which they seceded also suffered revival repercussions in southern Kentucky. In one sense the Presbyterian rupture in the Cumberland area traced back over half a century to the Old Side–New Side split that grew out of the first Great Awakening in the 1740s. There had been pro- and anti-revival parties within Presbyterianism ever since. Yet in a more immediate sense, the trouble in Cumberland came just after the Kentucky synod had been embroiled in the McNemar case. With obvious doctrinal revolt in the north, the careful synod was not about to allow any sort of deviation to occur in the south which might produce a second schism. The synod was prepared to use repression if necessary to preserve the status quo, and the application of restraining forces ironically provided just the soil for schism to proliferate.

It was in the Cumberland region of Kentucky that the Great Revival first appeared, and there under the labors of James McGready and his co-workers the revival persisted for several years with its fervor unabated. These Presbyterian friends of the awakening traced their theological lineage back to eighteenth-century New Side revivalists. With this background McGready and colleagues wholeheartedly approved of the multitude of conversions and looked for ways to keep the revival fires burning. Their first concern was to provide additional ministers to serve the new churches and enlarged congregations. The respected David Rice suggested an expedient remedy: the local presbytery should allow unordained "exhorters" and catechists (ministers-to-be) to perform semiclerical duties (excluding sacramental functions).

Rice's idea was not unprecedented, and the Transylvania Presbytery was open for innovations that would nurture the revival; so when four zealous men presented themselves "for the service of the church" at the October 1801 meeting of the presbytery, they were unhesitatingly appointed "to the business of exhortation and catechising." Yet trouble was brewing, for there was a vocal anti-revival minority in the Transylvania Presbytery which was determined that nothing out of the ordinary should occur; indeed, it already found scandalous the extraordinary events represented by camp-meeting revivalism. When at the next annual convening of the Transylvania Presbytery in October 1802 three of the young men on trial were, after examination, allowed actually to preach and fill church vacancies, five conservative ministers dissented from the presbytery's decision. A week after this decisive vote, the Synod of Kentucky met—with no representatives from the Transylvania Presbytery present—and proceeded to divide Transylvania into two separate entities, Transylvania and Cumberland presbyteries. This proved to be a fateful division, for the newly formed Cumberland Presbytery was equally split between pro- and anti-revival forces, but the friends of the revival, including McGready, were better organized and more determined. They quickly gained an upper hand. In fact, at the very first meeting of the presbytery, they accepted a former O'Kellyite Methodist as a fellow minister and established Methodist-like circuits to be supplied by unordained licentiates. To the conservatives, the revival spirit clearly seemed to be getting out of hand.

No one from the embroiled Cumberland Presbytery journeyed to Lexington for the 1803 meeting of the synod, but at the 1804 meeting in Danville a tenacious revival foe presented a letter detailing the complaints of the anti-revival forces. He in no uncertain terms warned ominously that the Cumberland Presbytery was improperly ordaining ministers by ignoring educational qualifications and not requiring rigid acceptance of the Westminster Confession of Faith. He had a case, for the revival forces were more concerned with a preacher's ability to gain converts than to quote the classics, and in the midst of revival success they had disregarded strict creedal requirements as practically irrelevant. Despite the modicum of truth in the charges, since there were Presbyterian precedents for such bending of the rules, nothing probably would have come of the complaints had these been normal times. But of course 1804 was assuredly not a normal time for the beleaguered Kentucky synod.

Fresh in the mind of every synod member was the Richard McNemar affair. Because of lack of supervision and the virtual freedom to experiment theologically, McNemar, Stone, and others had split away from the Presbyterian church, rejected the Confession of Faith, and were now on religious adventures that the synod dreaded to contemplate. In the face of their recent experience with doctrinal and ecclesiastical aberration, the synod was cautious. The Kentucky Presbyterian establishment was solidifying its position, regularizing its requirements, crushing even the intimation of internal subversion. Identifying the commotion in Cumberland with the rebellion by McNemar and Stone, the synod was panic-stricken. Finis Ewing, one of the revivalists whose credentials were disputed, later recalled that it was "only by confounding the revival with the New Light excitement—against the errors of which these good men [comprising the Kentucky synod] were battling with all their might—that the anti-revivalists gained their full confidence; and when this was done, an extension of their abhorrence of the latter to the former also was the natural consequence."

Perturbed and united, the orthodox center of the synod overreacted to what in reality should have been a minor incident. The synod appointed a committee of five conservatives to attend the next meeting of the Cumberland Presbytery. Only one dared to come, but the indignant presbytery denounced what they considered the high-handed nature of the synod investigation. At the 1805 meeting of the Kentucky synod another committee carefully went over the Cumberland minutes and labeled them "extremely defective." Consequently the synod appointed an even more conservative committee to inquire into the Cumberland proceedings. The synod was motivated by a sense of urgency and rectitude. "The object before the Synod was to suppress the growing irregularities in the west," it officially recorded, "and yet save one of her Presbyteries from disruption and final ruin."

Hence the synod moved with a heavy hand to squelch the possibility of another disastrous schism. The local presbytery, protective of its autonomy over issues such as ordination of ministers, fought what to it seemed the inquisitional attitude of the synod. As the controversy dragged on for several years, the squabble became acrimonious, with each side growing more self-righteously indignant. The synod's insistence that it had the power to dictate presbyterial matters drove the revival leaders away from the constituted authority of the Presbyterian church. The synod grew more aggressive, the presbytery reacted by becoming more defensive, and eventual schism was the result.

By 1809 when it was obvious that unless the presbytery gave in it would no longer be able to remain a constituent of the Kentucky synod of the Presbyterian church, several of the revival leaders including James McGready relented and reluctantly returned to the Presbyterian fold. Others more adamant in their belief that the synod had acted dictatorially refused to submit. Among this group, revivalists like Finis Ewing were less concerned about developing a new theological position than the old freedom to deviate somewhat without the repressive hand of the synod. Contending that "there are a number of ministers who are kept in the bosom of the Presbyterian church, who have deviated infinitely more from the confession than we have done," the remaining revivalists formally broke away from the synod, declared their ecclesiastical independence in 1810, and organized the Cumberland Presbyterian Church. The new denomination adopted a confession of faith and a discipline in 1816. Relaxing the emphasis on educational requirements for ministers, zealously committing themselves to evangelism, and softening the Calvinist notion of election, the Cumberland Presbyterian Church led by Finis Ewing enjoyed substantial success. By 1850 it numbered approximately 75,000, largely the result of orthodox overreaction to religious improvisation.

In the unexpected way history has of working itself out, the Great Revival instead of ushering in a glorious season of religious harmony and unity soon began to produce new pressures for change and conformity that splintered the Presbyterians. The Disciples of Christ and the Cumberland Presbyterians drew thousands of converts from the Presbyterian church, causing the parent body to increase very slowly. The Shakers never had substantial numerical growth, but as a novel example of communal living attracted much attention. The followers of Alexander Campbell caused great disruption in the Baptist churches too, though not to the degree the Presbyterians had been disturbed. The religious life of antebellum Kentucky was far more diverse, complex, and competitive after the Great Revival. The various groups, struggling for members and issuing pamphlets and broadsides defending their positions, made for a strenuous, active religious life. Kentucky was no longer the "dark and bloody ground," but peacefully the various faiths made their presence known. There was such pronounced religious concern in Kentucky that the author of a travel book in 1817 which covered six states and five territories in the nation's heartland found the vigorous religious life only in Kentucky worthy of mentioning.

4

CATHOLICISM

O<small>F ALL THE STORIES</small> of the religious groups that helped tame frontier Kentucky, that of the Catholic settlers and priests is perhaps the most unexpected and certainly the most remarkable. As Baltimore was the mother of the Catholic church in America, so was Bardstown, Kentucky, the mother of the Catholic church west of the Appalachians. But in ways no one could have foreseen, events transpiring thousands of miles away in France had an immeasurable impact on the future of Kentucky Catholicism. The anticlerical furor of the French Revolution all but destroyed the Catholic establishment in France; as a result, dozens of learned, sophisticated French priests and seminarians fled to safety. Many came to serve their church in America, where Bishop John Carroll, who until 1808 counted the entire nation as his see, sent many of these dedicated European emigrés to the Kentucky frontier. France's woe proved to be Kentucky's advantage, for the pioneer priests built cathedrals, colleges, and convents in the wilderness.

Among the earliest settlers who came to Kentucky in 1775 were the William Coomes family from Maryland and a Dr. Hart from Ireland. Hart, who practiced medicine and was probably the first physician in the territory, was a Catholic layman. The Coomes were also Catholic, and since Mrs. Coomes opened an elementary school in Harrodstown soon after arriving, she probably was the first schoolteacher in the region. But there were to be no Catholic settlements in Kentucky, no chapels, not even a priest, for another decade.

Catholics had lived in Maryland for a century and a half and like most Marylanders spent much of that time raising tobacco. At the close of the Revolution in 1783, many whose soils were exhausted from the unremitting planting of the pungent weed began to cast longing eyes toward the land of legendary fertility in Kentucky. General economic conditions combined with the constant threat of religious persecution played a minor role, but the persuasive argument was the promise of bountiful acres across the mountains. Consequently beginning in 1785 groups of Catholic families, united for protection and community, sold their Maryland properties and journeyed westward. As Catholic laymen they planted settlements in Nelson and later Scott counties, which eventually became the centers of Kentucky Catholicism. During the next decade emigration from Maryland continued, despite the hardships involved. As one Kentucky Catholic wrote to his sister in Maryland: "You say you could wish yourself, at times, in this country, but the reflections on moving extricates all notions of this kind. I must confess to you that it is a great undertaking, but not so bad as you imagine. If you was to see the luxurious soil of Kentucky I think it would raise an ambition in your mind that would surmount all difficulties."

According to tradition the early Maryland emigrants to Kentucky tried to arrange for a priest to accompany them; if so, their inability to secure one was understandable, for the infant Catholic church in America was drastically understaffed. For approximately 25,000 American Catholics there were only twenty-five priests; none could be released from his assigned duties to migrate westward. But at almost the same time the Maryland migration began, John Carroll of Baltimore in 1784 became the prefect apostolic with the authority to send priests wherever they were most needed. At the top of his priorities was the desire to find a clergyman for the developing communities in the West. Two years passed before Carroll found a priest for Kentucky, the Reverend Charles Maurice Whelan, an Irish Capuchin, and he proved to be unsatisfactory. Arriving in Kentucky in early 1787, Whelan visited the various Catholic communities and administered the sacraments in private homes or "church stations." Many of the Kentucky Catholics were obviously as worldly as their Protestant neighbors and resented the priest's attempts at discipline. When he refused to accept pay in the form of produce, a bitter argument erupted. Whelan was subsequently indicted for slander. It was for the good of all concerned when this first priest to Kentucky left in the spring of 1790.

A few months later another missionary, the Reverend William de Rohan, immigrated to Kentucky with a group of settlers from North Carolina. De Rohan had served in the backcountry of Virginia and North Carolina, and since he had been given permission to administer the sacraments in western Virginia, with Kentucky being the westernmost part of Virginia at the time, he assumed the prerogative of ministering to Kentucky. For three years, 1791–1794, he said Masses, witnessed marriages, and performed baptisms among the Catholics in Nelson and Scott counties. Within two years the first Catholic church was erected in Kentucky. Located in Nelson County, it was an unpretentious log cabin with a rudely carved altar, but, primitive though it was, it was the progenitor of many subsequent and far more elaborate churches. Unfortunately de Rohan was unsatisfactory because of a certain undependability perhaps rooted in alcoholism.

Back in Baltimore, Bishop Carroll continued to look for priests to send to the frontier. Just at this crucial juncture the terrors of the French Revolution provided a life-giving infusion of new ministerial talent for Carroll's huge see. The Reverend James Andrew Emery was the superior of the Seminary of Saint Sulpice in Paris, which was threatened with imminent destruction. He sought a place of refuge for his society somewhere in the New World, and with the establishment of the Diocese of Baltimore in 1789, he determined to locate a seminary in Baltimore if the new bishop, John Carroll, would consent. Carroll came to England in 1790 for his consecration; while there, Emery offered to erect a seminary in Carroll's Baltimore. Carroll was somewhat hesitant. He wondered if his fledgling see was mature enough to support a seminary and whether a seminary would threaten his favored Georgetown College. Emery was so determined that he sent Francis Charles Nagot, vice president of the Seminary of Saint Sulpice, to London to convince Carroll of the advantages of their proposal. Nagot made Carroll an attractive offer: the Sulpicians would provide the funds, the teachers, even the first students. Carroll was persuaded, and as a consequence in the spring of 1791 Nagot, the Reverends John Mary Tessier, Anthony Garnier, Michael Levadoux, and five seminarians set out for Baltimore. Arriving at their new home in July, they promptly purchased "The One Mile Tavern," several surrounding acres, and began Saint Mary's Seminary. This proved to be a turning point in the history of American Catholicism, for the steady stream of talented French priests who came to Baltimore as a result were gradually sent out across the nation, giving a recognizable Gallic flavor to the first half-century of American Catholicism.

Saint Mary's Seminary was a magnet for emigré European clergy, and less than a year after its founding, on March 29, 1792, three more priests—the Reverends J. B. Chicoisneau, John B. M. David, and Benedict Joseph Flaget—arrived, bringing with them two seminarians, Stephen T. Badin and N. Barret. These arrivals were to have a profound impact on Kentucky, for Flaget was to become the first bishop of the new see headquartered in Bardstown, David was to establish Kentucky's first Catholic seminary and found the Sisters of Charity of

55

Nazareth, and Badin was to be the real Father of Catholicism in Kentucky.

Stephen Theodore Badin was born in Orléans, France, in 1768, and except for the French Revolution no doubt would have died not far from his birthplace. In 1789 he entered the seminary run by the Sulpicians in Orléans. By 1791, however, the Revolution was at its height, and the seminary was forced to close. Consequently the young student transferred more than 3,000 miles to the new Saint Mary's Seminary in Baltimore to finish his studies. On May 25, 1793, Carroll ordained Badin a priest in the first such ceremony conducted in the United States. After his ordination Badin spent three months at Georgetown College studying English. Carroll had a task in mind for the new priest, for the bishop had not forgotten the desperate straits of Catholic settlers in Kentucky. Following Carroll's orders, on September 3, 1793, young Badin with a much older priest, the Reverend Michael Bernard Barrières, set out for the new state. The two walked as far as Pittsburgh and then by flatboat floated down the Ohio to Gallipolis; from there they walked until they reached Lexington at the end of November 1793. The next Sunday Badin said his first Mass in Kentucky, launching a ministerial career that made him to Kentucky Catholicism what Francis Asbury was to American Methodism. The hardships and primitive life of frontier society proved too much for the elderly Barrières, and within four months he left Kentucky. De Rohan, whose authority and character in Kentucky was suspect, ceased his ministry and soon moved on. Badin remained as the only priest for several hundred miles; the Reverend John Rivet at Post Vincennes in the Indiana Territory was the nearest brother. They often corresponded, but welcome letters have never been a substitute for companionship. Badin struggled on, lonely yet with unflagging zeal. So alone was Badin in Kentucky that to see him was a novelty for Protestants who had only heard rumors of "papists." Sometimes they would hide behind their walls and peep at him as he rode by, as if frightened by his suspected opulence. Then came Badin on horseback, simply dressed, and they were no doubt disappointed at the absence of spectacle.

There were at the time perhaps 300 Catholic families in all Kentucky, some in Scott County, most in Nelson County, and others scattered about. The first year and a half Badin resided in Scott County, even completing a chapel near Georgetown, but, since most of his parishioners were in Nelson County, Badin decided to change his residence. Subsequently he built himself a log cabin on Pottinger's Creek in Nelson County, where the first substantial Catholic emigrants from Maryland had settled. Badin's home was popularly called "Priestland," though he named it after his patron, Saint Stephen. Three miles away was Sacred Heart Chapel, which had been erected by de Rohan in 1792. During these early years Badin's ministry was comparable to that of a Methodist itinerant. Since there were only two chapels, most Catholics had to worship in private homes, and Badin traveled hundreds of miles to reach the widely scattered stations. Badin heard confessions, celebrated Mass, baptized children, witnessed marriages, taught catechism, cared for the sick—in short, he did whatever his people needed. The roads were hardly more than trails, most rivers were unbridged, and Catholic families were far apart. Simply journeying to the various families was a rigorous task that would have disheartened most men. To make matters worse, Badin was forced by circumstances to live in unremitting poverty—a far cry from what he might reasonably have expected as a young student at Orléans. But hardships never daunted Badin's determination to minister where he saw religious needs. His own comfort and health were sacrificed for his mission. As he wrote Bishop Carroll once, "No clergyman is fit for Kentucky who seeks for his interests more than for those of Jesus Christ."

Though Badin was as headstrong as he was zealous, he quickly recognized that there was no way he could adequately serve such a huge empire as he was assigned; indeed, it was larger than all France. Over and over he wrote Carroll, outlining the needs and promise of Kentucky, importuning him for pastoral help. Carroll did the best he could, and when the Reverend Michael Fournier, another French refugee, arrived in Baltimore, the bishop sent him to Kentucky in the fall of 1796. After a brief period to become acclimated to the conditions of life in the backcountry, Fournier gave welcome assistance to the overworked Badin. The two divided the state, each ministering to his region. In January 1799 another French emigré, the Reverend Anthony Salmon, arrived in Kentucky, and he stayed in Bardstown to help Badin. A month later the Reverend John Thayer from Massachusetts also came to Kentucky. That autumn, however, Salmon died from injuries suffered in falling from his horse. Badin was disconsolate, yet he could take comfort in the knowledge that Fournier still served faithfully the growing Catholic population of the state. Suddenly in February 1803 Fournier died. To make matters worse, Thayer was unpopular and ineffective. He was a poor horseman, a severe liability in Kentucky, and his Federalist and abolitionist views did not endear him to the Kentuckians. He departed the state in 1803. Once more Badin was left alone, with perhaps a thousand Catholic families to care for, and the nearest fellow priests were Rivet at Post Vincennes (who died in February 1804), the Reverend Donatien Olivier in Illinois, and the Reverend Gabriel Richard in Michigan. After a decade of laboring in Kentucky, Badin still faced what must at times have seemed an impossible ministry.

During the worst of times Badin struggled on, keeping lit the scattered embers of Catholic faith. Of particular importance in a state where Catholics were a distinct minority, Badin, educated, witty, and socially adept, was on very friendly terms with many of the leading Protestants of the state. At times in fact he seemed to get along better with the Protestants than with his own people. The good relations between Catholics and Protestants he established set the tone for the subsequent years, despite occasional outbreaks of unchristian bigotry. Yet Badin never soft-pedaled his beliefs; to the contrary, he was quick to defend his faith and vigorous in argument. Such aggressiveness gained him favor, for Kentuckians disliked lukewarmness in religion or politics. He even had published in Bardstown in 1805 an edition of *Real Principles of Roman Catholics,* to which he had added extensive notes; that was the first Catholic work printed in the West. Several years later he printed another pamphlet, *Summary Proofs of the Catholic Doctrine.* Both of these pioneer works of apologetics were closely based on prior works by other authors, but Badin made them widely available in Kentucky. He also ridiculed the Great Revival, warning Catholics not to be misled by the "noise."

Badin was as stern and rigid as he was energetic, and he often found his views on the life of faith greatly at variance with those of most of his parishioners. He taught young catechumens with a severe strictness and never missed a chance to exhort families to have morning and evening prayers. He expected his people to live devoutly, and they sometimes resented his exactions. As a result he was more respected than loved. His opposition to dancing, a pastime popular among all Kentuckians, became legendary. Like a bloodhound, he could sniff out dancing schools and private parties, and he particularly disliked dancing on the night before the Sabbath. Coming to a community on Saturday expecting to hear confessions and catechize the children before Sunday Mass, he found the people's excited anticipation of a Saturday night dance more than his meager patience could stand. As a contemporary wrote, "He sometimes arrived unexpectedly at a house, in the evening, while dancing was going on, glided into the room before any one perceived it, and told them smiling, 'that it was time for night prayers'. . . . most of the merry dancers generally effected their escape before the close of the evening devotions." Badin's detestation of dancing was an eccentricity, one that makes him more human, and while we might smile today at his concerns, contemporaries were sure to watch their behavior when they knew he was likely to be lurking near.

In 1805 Badin gained clerical assistance in the person of the Reverend Charles Nerinckx, a native of Belgium and another victim of the French Revolution. They immediately became close friends, and as a tandem the itinerant priests continued more effectively the lonely ministry Badin had begun. Nerinckx had arrived in Baltimore in November 1804 and was sent by Bishop Carroll to Georgetown College to learn English. Carroll already envisioned the sturdy Belgian serving on the Kentucky frontier, so in the spring of 1805 Nerinckx began his journey west with a band of Trappist monks also headed for Kentucky and a prospective monastery in Washington County. The Trappists, who moved at a deliberate pace without speaking, were too slow for the vigorous Nerinckx, so in Bedford, Pennsylvania, he bought a horse and rode on ahead, reaching Kentucky several months before the meditative monks.

Upon Nerinckx's arrival in Bardstown, Badin was ecstatic. During the first winter the two priests traveled together throughout Kentucky, going from mission station to mission station, as Badin introduced Nerinckx to the Kentuckians and the congregations to their new priest. After this tour Nerinckx was given charge of six of Badin's fifteen congregations. Even though the Belgian continued to live with Badin until 1812, the two were so often on horseback administering the sacraments to far-flung congregations that they seldom saw each other. Often like Methodists they had to preach outdoors, and they arranged schedules in advance for officiating at the various Catholic stations. They appointed catechists at each station to supervise religious instruction between visits of the priests. Nerinckx, short and stocky, had immense physical strength and stamina. He rode so often and long that two horses were necessary to keep him mounted. Although he was like Badin an exceedingly strict disciplinarian and an inveterate foe of dancing, he was widely loved by the people. He put great emphasis upon confession, organized a number of devotional societies such as a Confraternity of the Rosary, and gathered numbers of Catholic families into churches. He erected ten new churches, his robust strength inspiring the other laborers.

But Kentucky Catholics most treasured Nerinckx for his wonderful way with children. In this attribute he was a perfect complement to Badin, who once confessed to Carroll that "the children are my Cross, instead of my crown." Nerinckx on the other hand found in the young faces his greatest joy, and his obvious love for them kindled in the children a mutual love for Nerinckx. He organized classes for learning the catechism and awarded prizes to the most deserving. In building numerous churches and awakening the faith of children, Nerinckx did much to insure the future growth of Kentucky Catholicism. As Bishop Martin John Spalding concluded, "Badin had laid the foundation; and, like a skillful architect, [Nerinckx] reared the superstructure."

Nerinckx had been in Kentucky several months when the Trappists finally arrived in Louisville in the fall of 1805, exhausted and many of them sick with the fever. This colony of contemplative monks had left Amsterdam in 1803, then after a few months in Baltimore established a short-lived school at Pigeon Hill, Pennsylvania, while the Reverend Urbain Guillet, their superior, and another brother came to Kentucky in the summer of 1804 looking for a site for their planned monastery. They chose a location on Pottinger's Creek, and Guillet returned to Pennsylvania to guide the colony to their new home. When the slow-moving, bedraggled caravan finally arrived in Louisville, the local Catholics met them and conveyed them by wagon to their proposed new home.

Badin and Nerinckx knew that these closely cloistered men would be of no help in their day-by-day ministry, but they hoped the Trappists would establish schools, improve by example the neighboring religious life, and provide a place of quiet retreat for the weary secular priests. They did open almost immediately the first Kentucky school under Catholic auspices, bought additional land, and set up a clock and watch works. But the rigorous life of asceticism which the Trappists practiced rendered them physically unfit for the rugged life of backcountry Kentucky. They observed "perpetual silence," slept on boards with a single blanket for covering and a rough canvas bag for a pillow, and their schedule allowed them only four hours daily for sleep. With the plainest food set at their table, and a severe fast from Easter to Ascension day, they lived a simple life of penance and prayer. Such a regimen, however conducive to holiness, left them tired and sickly. In 1808 their establishment suffered a disastrous fire, and Guillet began to make plans to leave. With great effort they constructed a huge flatboat and during the high water in the spring of 1809 floated down the river systems until they reached a site a few miles north of Saint Louis. Here at Monk's Mound they tried once more to establish a monastery. Yet again they met disappointment, finally returning in 1813 to France, their American mission a failure. Almost thirty years later, in 1848, the Trappists returned to the United States and in Nelson County established Gethsemani, the first abbey in the New World. Conditions by then had changed enough to allow their austere community to survive, and they subsequently built a beautiful monastery.

Another order of priests, the Dominicans, were introduced to Kentucky in 1805. The Reverend Edward Fenwick, born of prominent parents in Saint Mary's County, Maryland, had been sent to Europe for his education. After graduating from Holy Cross College in Belgium, he had entered the Dominican order. It too was disrupted by the French Revolution, and Fenwick began to make plans for a Dominican house in the United States, preferably in Maryland. The Dominican general and Bishop Carroll approved the idea, so Fenwick and three volunteers came to Maryland, with Fenwick and the Reverend Robert Angier arriving in November 1804. Carroll then used his persuasive abilities and clerical authority to convince Fenwick to found their house in Kentucky, which hungered for priests. In the summer of 1805 Fenwick visited Kentucky looking for a proper location; Badin gave advice and offered warm encouragement. Fenwick discovered a region to his liking and returned to Baltimore where Angier had been joined by the other two Dominican volunteers, the Reverends Samuel T. Wilson and William R. Tuite.

Wilson and Tuite very soon set out for Kentucky, and by spring of 1806 they were busy in their religious duties, already beginning to educate youths in their home. Fenwick was delayed in Maryland selling his estate; after his arrival in July the Dominicans began looking for a permanent site. Using Fenwick's inheritance, they purchased a plantation near Springfield and began constructing buildings, naming their home Saint Rose of Lima, the mother house of the Dominican order in this nation. In 1808 Saint Rose's Church was begun, and a college, Saint Thomas Aquinas, was opened. The small college flourished, for even Protestant parents respected the moral discipline and the polished classics offered by the teaching fathers. The Kentucky Catholics looked forward to the day when Kentucky-born and -educated priests could fill clerical positions.

The Dominican fathers were popular, for they were not nearly so strict as Badin and Nerinckx; the Dominicans even approved of social dancing. Badin and Nerinckx were scandalized by what they considered the Dominicans' lack of rigor and sent a steady barrage of complaining letters to Bishop Carroll. Since Badin had first received Fenwick with great happiness, it was perhaps Nerinckx who helped turn him against the Dominicans.

Yet Badin and Nerinckx were two of a kind; very possibly their austerity can be traced to their education in France and Belgium, where the clergy were "considerably tainted by the Jansenistic teachings," a doctrinal system of ultra-Calvinistic rigor. The Dominicans for their part were amazed at the strictness of Badin and Nerinckx. Both sides undoubtedly exaggerated the other's perceived faults, and Carroll fortunately had the good sense and conciliatory skill to preserve an unsteady truce between the priests. Fenwick led the Dominicans with great dexterity, making their name a byword for kindness, good teaching, and piety among Catholics in the Midwest. Their leniency—in keeping with Kentucky mores—combined with Fenwick's native Americanism to make the Dominicans very popular. Fenwick pioneered Catholic expansion into neighboring Ohio, eventually being named the first bishop of Cincinnati in 1821.

In the years after 1805 the Catholic population of Kentucky increased steadily as a result of internal growth, migration from Maryland, and later a surge of Irish and German immigrants who came down the Ohio River to booming Louisville. Even as early as 1792 Carroll had wanted to subdivide his huge see, but the papal authorities hesitated. They recognized, however, that the rapid growth of the new nation eventually would require new dioceses. To that effect they requested reports from Carroll in 1802 and 1806 concerning possible future sees and bishops. When asked for information, Badin in 1804 advocated the creation of a western see established in Bardstown, "the heart of the Catholic settlements." After the arrival of Nerinckx, the Trappists, and the Dominicans, it was evident that new organizational arrangements would soon be required. Carroll began to consider potential bishops, writing for information and advice, and the laymen of Kentucky became anxious. A great many feared that Badin, as vicar general already the local administrator of the church in Kentucky, would be the choice; although they respected him, they strongly opposed his rigidity, exacting discipline, implacable opposition to dancing, and his tendency to be contentious. Badin had the good judgment to recognize his liabilities and the needs of Kentucky. In 1807 he journeyed to Baltimore to talk to Carroll and to recommend that the Reverend Benedict Joseph Flaget be appointed as Kentucky's first bishop if approved by Rome.

Carroll agreed with Badin (he had no doubt come to his conclusion even before talking with the Kentuckian) and awaited the action of the Holy See. Finally in 1808 word came from Rome; Baltimore had been made an archdiocese, with suffragan sees established at Boston, New York, Philadelphia, and Bardstown. Flaget was appointed bishop of Kentucky. His see, the region north of the southern boundary of Tennessee and east of the Mississippi River, reaching all the way to Canada, was a vast territory, with problems to match its promise, but Flaget was a perfect choice for the troublesome duty. Badin was pleased to be relieved of his supervisory duties, and the Catholic laymen of Kentucky were joyous.

Benedict Joseph Flaget, a Sulpician, was born and educated in France. In 1792 he came to Baltimore in company with Badin and the Reverend John Baptist David, and almost immediately Flaget was sent to the frontier garrison of Post Vincennes. Thus he experienced American frontier conditions even before Badin did, serving two and a half years in the Indiana Territory. Then he was called to Georgetown College, where he taught geography and French for several years. Flaget in 1798–1801 went to Cuba to organize a college, following which he returned to Baltimore assuming he would spend the rest of his days teaching at Saint Mary's Seminary and College. Thus it was as a priest of wide experience and strong constitution that Flaget was appointed the bishop of Kentucky. At first, news of the appointment flabbergasted, then overwhelmed him. A man of great humility, Flaget was genuinely concerned that he did not possess enough theological ability to serve in so important a post. He begged Carroll to recall the appointment, and when Carroll—an excellent judge of men—refused, the distraught Flaget traveled to France to try to persuade Emery, the superior general of the Society of Saint Sulpice, to aid him in entreating Rome. When Flaget saw Emery, the superior general's first words were, "My Lord, you should have been already in your diocese, the Pope has given you an express order to accept." There was no escape, so Flaget concluded some private business matters in Europe, returned to America, and entered upon a spiritual retreat of forty days in preparation for the work. On November 4, 1810, Carroll (now archbishop) with the newly appointed bishops of Philadelphia and Boston consecrated Flaget in Saint Patrick's Church at Fells Point, an older section of Baltimore.

The Catholic Church in America was so poor that Flaget had to wait six months until a subscription among his friends provided funds to enable him and his party to go to Kentucky. Accompanying him were a priest from Canada, a subdeacon, two young women intending to join a religious order, and his old and dear friend, John Baptist David. David had been a companion of Flaget and Badin on the ship from France some twenty years earlier. Emery, knowing David's talents and suspecting Kentucky's needs, had already encouraged him to be the superior of the seminary Flaget planned to establish in his new see. In addition David was to be Flaget's closest associate, adviser, and confidant in Kentucky. The impoverished little band made its way west. Flaget was penniless and without a home, with no property, and surely depressed when, on June 4, 1811, they arrived at Louisville. Nerinckx met them and escorted the group to Bardstown, where a large crowd, including most of the Catholic clergy in Kentucky, turned out to greet their new bishop. There in a lovely outdoors setting Flaget offered his first Mass and gave Holy Communion to his congregation. A new era in Kentucky Catholicism had begun, even though Flaget for his first year had to live under crowded conditions in a log cabin. Badin called him "the poorest Bishop in the Christian world." A tall, striking man, of sweet disposition in contrast to Badin, Flaget was a welcome sight to his clergy and flock.

With the arrival of Flaget in Bardstown in 1811, Kentucky Catholicism entered a new era. David had come west with his bishop to organize a seminary, which he did aboard a flatboat as he, Flaget, and three students traveled to Louisville. After arriving in Kentucky the peripatetic seminary settled in Marion County at Saint Stephen's, Badin's home. In 1818 Saint Thomas's Seminary, as it was named, moved to Nelson County near Bardstown, where a plot of land had been donated. Moreover, Flaget wanted his supporting clergy and seminaries near the see city of his diocese. In 1819, after the cathedral was opened in Bardstown, the seminarians moved to a new major seminary, Saint Joseph's, adjacent to the cathedral. Saint Thomas's thereafter was a preparatory seminary. In conjunction with the Dominican-founded Saint Thomas Aquinas College, Kentuckians could now expect home-grown priests. Not the least of the contributions of the seminaries was the acculturation to American mores of the continuing stream of European priests. David and Flaget had been in the United States for twenty years and had learned American ways, and this they taught in addition to theology.

Meanwhile, Nerinckx, who had long been an advocate of devotional societies and the teaching of children, in 1812 succeeded in founding the Sisters of Loretto, a sisterhood devoted to the Christian education of girls. Wearing homespun black habits, going barefoot except in winter, rising early and eating the plainest food, the Sisters of Loretto nevertheless flourished and attracted many members. By 1824 they numbered more than one hundred and operated six schools. Only a few months after their founding, David at Saint Thomas's Seminary organized a similar order, the Sisters of Charity. Their asceticism was less rigid, but they too educated poor children and cared for the sick. Located at first near Saint Stephen's, they moved their motherhouse to another site (called Nazareth) near Bardstown in 1822.

Despite a running argument with Badin over the ownership of church property, Flaget could take comfort in the progress of his faith. In 1815 he reported to the pope that in Kentucky he had ten priests, nineteen churches, perhaps 10,000 Catholic laity, two sisterhoods, a seminary, and a college operated by the Dominicans. Already Flaget was planning the construction of a cathedral in Bardstown to be the shrine of the West. After tireless fund-raising Flaget was able to lay the cornerstone in 1816, twenty-nine years after Whelan introduced Catholicism to Kentucky. The cathedral, 120 feet in length, 74 feet wide, with a steeple reaching 150 feet, was monumental. It was equipped with a large bell from France, a worthy organ, two paintings procured in Belgium by Nerinckx, and splendid ornaments including golden candlesticks and richly embroidered vestments for the priests. Catholicism had come a long way since the log chapels of Badin's early years, and to commemorate the maturation of the Kentucky church, at the service of consecration of the cathedral on August 8, 1819, Robert A. Abell—the first native Kentuckian ordained to the Catholic priesthood—gave the major sermon. He concluded his memorable address on this signal occasion by thanking "those who had enabled the Bishop to erect, in a country but lately overshadowed by interminable forests, a cathedral church that would be honorable to the Catholic faith of any people."

In many ways the growth of early Kentucky Catholicism was directly related to Catholic difficulties in Europe. But the European connection to Kentucky did not end with the defeat of Napoleon, for the Kentucky clergy still had their European contacts. Nowhere can this be better illustrated than by the story of the French

Jesuits in Kentucky. Even before there were Jesuits in the state, however, Nerinckx was to alter significantly the Jesuit presence in the United States. For more than a century there had been a few Jesuits in the nation, for the Reverend Andrew White who landed in Maryland aboard the *Ark* in 1634 was a member of the Society of Jesus and began the Jesuit missions there. Yet prejudice toward the order forced them to minimize their affiliation, and after Pope Clement XIV suppressed the Society of Jesus administratively in 1773, the Jesuits became nonexistent by name in this country. When Pius VII in 1814 reestablished the order, America was in great need of energetic missionaries. No one recognized this more than the overburdened Kentucky priests. Bishop Flaget in 1815 promptly appealed to John Anthony Grassi, the superior of the Jesuits in America, but Grassi had no one to send. The following year, Nerinckx journeyed to his homeland, Belgium, using the opportunity to publicize the ministerial needs of Kentucky. He eagerly sought the labors of Belgian Jesuits. Upon his return to America, Nerinckx brought eight Jesuit novitiates back to Georgetown. Returning to Belgium in 1820, he recruited another band of Jesuits who arrived in Kentucky in 1821. This group later traveled west to Missouri and began at Florissant in 1823 the great Jesuit mission in the Midwest. Saint Louis University is only one result of their activities. But Kentucky had to wait a decade longer before the Society of Jesus was established within its borders.

In 1828 Flaget began a concerted campaign to attract Jesuits to Kentucky, even offering them Saint Joseph's College (Seminary) in Bardstown. For several years his pleading letters were of no avail. Then once again European events proved fortuitous for Kentucky. The French government in 1828 banned Jesuits from teaching and, during the July 1830 revolution, expelled the Society of Jesus. Instructed by their French Provincial who had been in communication with Flaget, four of the exiled Jesuits set out for Kentucky. After spending the winter months of 1831 in New Orleans, two of them journeyed to Bardstown, arriving on May 14, 1831. They discovered that, although Flaget welcomed them, some of the other Catholic clergy were anything but happy to see Jesuits coming to Kentucky. Moreover, Saint Joseph's upon inspection seemed lacking in promise. Just when they were contemplating returning to New Orleans, the Reverend William Byrne wrote to Flaget offering to turn over to him Saint Mary's Seminary (which Byrne owned) near Bardstown so that Flaget could transfer it to the Jesuits. Saint Mary's future seemed bright; consequently not only were the two Jesuits authorized by their European superiors to stay in Kentucky but also three more Jesuits were sent to reinforce them, arriving in late 1832. Meanwhile two local clergy had applied for admission into the order. The Jesuit community was formally inaugurated on January 1, 1833, teaching assignments were made, and the Society of Jesus took charge of Saint Mary's.

At first Saint Mary's Seminary was primarily a secondary school; in 1837 it was chartered as a university and subsequently offered collegiate instruction. For a short time after 1839, when Flaget closed the minor seminary of Saint Thomas's, the Jesuits at Saint Mary's were contracted to teach the seminarians. Then for some reason Flaget's coadjutor, Bishop Guy Ignatius Chabrat, brusquely ordered the seminarians to leave. Nevertheless, the college prospered—it even had a system of elective courses—although by today's standards its enrollment, reaching a maximum of 127 in 1838, remained miniscule. While Saint Mary's was the center of Jesuit activities, they assisted neighboring clergy, offered retreats for them, and in other ways promoted the cause of their common faith.

The Reverend Peter Chazelle in 1839 broached a bold plan to Flaget to further the church in Kentucky. He suggested moving the see city from Bardstown to Louisville, clearly the leading city of the region. He also suggested establishing there a major regional seminary, staffed by the Jesuits, to serve the entire Midwest. Flaget liked both proposals and took Chazelle with him to Baltimore to present the plan to the Fourth Provincial Council. The council of bishops approved transferring the see to Louisville, but balked at moving the seminary. Flaget and Chabrat were not to be rebuffed, and the two Kentucky bishops continued to advocate the complete proposal even though Chazelle had meanwhile been replaced as superior of the Kentucky Jesuits. Chazelle seems not to have represented Jesuit opinion, for most of the Kentucky Jesuits thought the seminary should remain in Bardstown. But the Kentucky bishops intended at least to open a college in Louisville because they already had purchased property there, and they practically forced the Jesuits to staff it. With Chazelle gone and the other Jesuits hesitant to overextend the order, Flaget and Chabrat seemed to feel the Jesuits were reneging, since it was they who had proposed the seminary in the first place. Feeling pressured, the Reverend William Stack Murphy, Chazelle's successor, opened Saint Ignatius Literary Institution in 1842.

Flaget, over eighty years of age and possibly senile, now seemed to turn against the Jesuits, perhaps being prodded by Chabrat who had always harbored resentment against them. Saint Joseph's College in Bardstown had long been the apple of Flaget's eye, and for years he had hoped the Jesuits would take it over. It was for that purpose he had originally invited them to Kentucky. But the Jesuits had consistently refused to accept the unsuccessful college. Now, with Saint Ignatius Literary Institution beginning to prosper, Flaget viewed it as a threat to Saint Joseph's. Not only would Saint Ignatius attract students away from Saint Joseph's, but its growth meant the Jesuits would be even less likely to have men to spare for the other institution. Flaget's opposition to the Louisville school grew flagrant. When the Jesuits attempted to raise money to erect a much-needed building, Flaget and Chabrat refused to support their appeal. A war of nerves between the bishops and the Jesuits had erupted; clearly the Jesuits' future in Kentucky was limited. Subsequently on January 1, 1846, they announced they were withdrawing from Louisville and retreated to Bardstown. For a variety of reasons they had already begun to seek a new mission field, since Kentucky had not proved hospitable.

Meanwhile the Catholic population of New York City was increasing rapidly. Bishop John Hughes of New York enticed the Kentucky Jesuits to his diocese by offering them Saint John's College (now Fordham University) in a little village named Fordham, near New York. Consequently the Jesuits transferred Saint Mary's back to the diocese, sold their property, and by the summer of 1846 had begun their exodus from Kentucky. The Kentucky mission, founded by Jesuit exiles from France, had ended. Ironically two years later other Jesuits, from the vice-province of Missouri, reentered Kentucky, took over Saint Joseph's College, and prospered until they too, in a dispute with the bishop, left Kentucky in 1868.

The pioneers of the Catholic church in Kentucky all lived to a ripe old age. Flaget was bishop until his death in 1850, when he was succeeded by the Kentucky-born Martin John Spalding (1810–1872). David, after years of service as Flaget's coadjutor and brief service as ordinary, died in 1841, the year in which the see moved from Bardstown to the emerging city of Louisville. Badin, whose great work really ended with the coming of Flaget and who after 1819 traveled widely in Europe and wrote extensively, returned to spend his last years once more as an itinerant missionary priest. The octogenarian preached Flaget's burial sermon; Badin died three years later in 1853.

The brilliant Spalding was a worthy successor to Flaget. By birth he was related to the first Catholic settlers in Kentucky, had been inspired by Nerinckx and Flaget to enter the religious life, and after schooling in several Kentucky institutions—notably Saint Mary's College and Saint Joseph's Seminary, where he came into contact with David, Francis P. Kenrick (an unusually inspiring teacher, able apologist, and later bishop of Philadelphia and archbishop of Baltimore), and George Elder—Spalding was admitted to the prestigious Urban College of the Propaganda in Rome. He was the first American graduate of this institution and finished at the head of his class. When he returned to Kentucky in 1834, everyone anticipated great things from him, and Spalding more than lived up to expectations. A prolific writer, church historian, capable administrator, and inspiring bishop, Spalding led the Kentucky see with outstanding success from 1850 to 1864. Thereafter he became as archbishop of Baltimore the nation's leading Catholic apologist and legislator, and perhaps the greatest archbishop between John Carroll and James Cardinal Gibbons. That Kentucky within little more than fifty years after being organized as an impoverished see could furnish the American church with such an eminent archbishop is the most telling proof of the foundations laid by Badin and Flaget.

The see of Bardstown-Louisville played a significant role in the national expansion of the Catholic church; it was the stepping-stone by which Roman Catholicism spread throughout much of the Midwest. As an integral part of the American Catholic church, it also unhappily was beset with the troubles that plagued the national church, lay trusteeism and virulent nativism. According to canon law, the right of appointing and dismissing priests was totally that of the bishops; lay trustees had no say. Nevertheless, while at first all church property legally was in the name of the resident priest or bishop, gradually a system of lay trustees was developed in most American sees by which laymen participated in the financial affairs of the church. Since European immigration brought Catholics of various nationalities to America, the problem of lay choice of clergymen vexed the bishops.

The preponderance of early bishops was French, and as the German and Irish migration reached flood proportions, these Catholic newcomers wanted priests of their own nationality. The old-line French and English hierarchy, particularly the Sulpician archbishop Ambrose Maréchal and the English James Whitfield, were determined to limit the growth of an Irish hierarchy. In democratic Kentucky, the first state to remove property qualifications for voting, the indigenous Catholics shared the republican ideals of their neighbors. The Protestant mode of congregational autonomy was a definite threat to Catholic apostolicity. As early as 1807 Badin reported that there was a movement by the White Sulphur congregation "to establish a republican or Presbyterian constitution for the parish." Later he successfully opposed a similar threat on the part of Scott County Catholics. Such developments should not be surprising, for the Catholic church took on an American coloration, the Methodist-like itinerancy of Badin and Nerinckx being but one example. In the American environment Old World forms and procedures were difficult to maintain.

The lay trustee issue in its more common guise was not a major problem in Kentucky, but the choice of Guy Ignatius Chabrat as coadjutor of the see of Kentucky in 1832 resulted in a virtual uprising among the Kentucky priests. The problem had a tangled beginning. Flaget recognized that his current coadjutor, David, was enfeebled with age and asthma, and rather than risk embarrassing him by asking for his resignation, Flaget chose a disingenuous method of obtaining a younger assistant. He wrote to Rome complaining of his own ill health and recommended that Chabrat be authorized to grant Confirmation and in other ways help him. He mentioned that should Rome wish either of the two older men, he or David, to resign, he would gladly step down. Flaget thought Rome would simply grant Chabrat the desired authority and disregard the proffered resignations. But while Flaget, in David's sarcastic phrase, was "showing his *infirmity* by a journey of several hundred miles on horseback," astonishing news arrived in Bardstown: Flaget's resignation was accepted, the infirm David was raised to bishop, and Chabrat was named his coadjutor.

If Flaget was surprised and disturbed to hear the report, poor David was prostrated. The Kentucky Catholic community was outraged over the seemingly whimsical change of bishops. After a hurried conference Flaget wrote to Rome asking to be restored to his office, the shaken David sent his resignation, and Chabrat's status was left up to the Holy See. What upset the Catholic clergy was the knowledge not only that David was much more feeble than Flaget but also that Chabrat was a peculiarly unpopular French priest. The laity wanted an American bishop to succeed Flaget, one who could speak English fluently and give sermons as eloquent as the Protestant pulpit orators. Several of the priests were quite vocal in their opposition, writing of their concerns to Bishop Kenrick who forwarded their complaints to Rome. Others sent letters to the American students in Rome (including the future Bishop Spalding), who forwarded their views to the Propaganda. Four priests threatened to leave if Chabrat were made coadjutor; a petition signed by the Catholic women of Louisville asked plaintively, "must we have another Frenchman for bishop?" Rome in March 1833 had already accepted David's resignation and returned Flaget to his bishopric; Chabrat's appointment was negated. But while the Sacred Congregation received the views of those opposed to Chabrat, it also received the impassioned pleas of Flaget that Chabrat be named. Ultimately in the face of popular opposition Chabrat was chosen; the Kentuckians were crestfallen but bowed to the wishes of Rome. No priests left the diocese, and while Chabrat proved not to be as disastrous as the Americans feared, he was far from a loved and respected administrator. Sixteen of the most distinguished priests of the diocese even wrote Pope Gregory XVI a long letter in November 1835 detailing

75

Chabrat's limitations in office. The Propaganda urged calm and a reverent acceptance of the Holy See's decision. But years later when Chabrat resigned, Rome quickly chose an American, Martin John Spalding, as successor.

For a variety of reasons Protestant-Catholic relations were remarkably good in Kentucky for many decades. At first the number of Catholics was so small that never even in the mind of the most extreme nativist could they be considered a threat to Kentucky's democratic institutions. And most Kentucky Catholics were from respectable local families, descendants of the Maryland migrants of the late eighteenth and early nineteenth centuries. In no way, then, could Kentucky Catholics be categorized as a foreign presence. But as Louisville on the Ohio River grew into a leading American city, thousands of German and Irish immigrants came to swell the city's population. By 1855 over half the city's 60,000 inhabitants were foreign-born, and many were believed to be political radicals.

After the *Louisville Anzeizer* began publication in 1849, advocating editorially that immigrants retain their German language and customs, Protestants in Louisville grew alarmed. Then in 1853 when Bishop Spalding objected to the reading of the King James Version of the Bible in the public schools (he merely asked that Catholic children be permitted to use the Douay Version), many Protestants jumped to the conclusion that Catholics sought to undermine the Christian foundations of American society. There had been minor outbreaks of anti-Catholic sentiment in Louisville earlier, though nothing comparable to that which inflicted other sections of the nation. This heritage of coexistence lulled the *Louisville Catholic Telegraph and Advocate* in April 1853 to write: "The Catholic religion here occupies a higher place in public estimation, and such exhibitions of low bigotry as often disgrace the Eastern cities, and Cincinnati, would not be tolerated by public sentiment in cities of the South, and especially in Louisville." The relatively civilized past, however, served as no guide to the future, for to the Protestant majority the increasing foreign and Catholic element in Louisville boded ill. The Whig party was dying, and as its former adherents drifted into the nativistic Know-Nothing party, opportunistic politicians and editors exacerbated the real fears of many Protestants. The result was a period of anti-foreign and anti-Catholic hysteria in Louisville that culminated in the infamous "Bloody Monday" of August 6, 1855.

Nationally a series of nativist riots followed in the wake of a tour in 1853 by Archbishop Gaetano Bedini, ostensibly the papal nuncio to Brazil. Fanatics thought his trip was preparatory to a papal takeover, and he was preceded by an extremist ex-priest, Giacinto Achilli, who portrayed Bedini as the "Bloody Butcher of Bologna." In Louisville nothing worse happened than jeers and the burning in effigy of the nuncio, but it was an omen of things to come. In January 1855 the belligerent Achilli gave at the Louisville YMCA an impassioned series of addresses, the first of which was ominously billed as "Popery Opposed to Civil and Religious Liberty." Spalding felt constrained to offer rebuttal in a temperate and well-attended lecture series entitled "Popular Prejudice against the Catholic Church." Clearly the nativist issue was on the public mind.

After Louisville elected a Know-Nothing mayor in April 1855, the editor of the *Louisville Journal*, George Prentice, read the signs of the times and became a virulent supporter of nativism. In sensationalist terms he denounced the Catholics, writing that now was the time "to grapple with the foreign hordes." He pictured the Catholics as minions of a diabolical pope who plotted the overthrow of republican institutions. Warning of the insidious dangers of the foreign "peril," Prentice on July 4, 1855, advocated that "Americans should rule America." In the context of rising tensions, such irresponsible journalism bears much blame for what happened. "So go ahead Know-Nothings," Prentice had proclaimed, "and raise just as big a storm as you please." On election morning, Monday, August 6, 1855, Prentice urged Protestants to "Rally to put down an organization of Jesuit Bishops, Priests, and other Papists, who aim by secret oaths and horrid perjuries, and midnight plottings, to sap the foundation of all our political edifices—state and national." Much of the public took these warnings to heart. Consequently on election day, Know-Nothing hoodlums patrolled the polls, "protecting" democracy from peacefully voting foreign-born citizens. Anger, fear, and frustration broke down better judgment, and the result was a day of terror. Mobs roamed the streets, assaulting German and Irish citizens. From a German ward came gunshots aimed toward nativists; a row of Irish homes was burned. Bullies were given license to maul, and both sides fought with abandon. Bishop Spalding gave the keys of the Catholic cathedral to the mayor, putting the burden of its protection on the civil authorities; otherwise much Catholic property might have been destroyed. When the furor finally subsided, twenty-two lay dead and countless others were wounded. "We have just passed through a reign of terror," wrote a saddened Spalding a few days later.

Spalding's response was one of courage: moderation and restraint. Two days after "Bloody Monday" he had a statement published in the *Daily Louisville Democrat* that concluded with these words: "I entreat all to pause and reflect, to commit no violence which they would regret in cooler moments; to believe no idle rumor, and to cultivate that peace and love which are the characteristics of the religion of Christ. We are to remain on earth but a few years; let us not add to the necessary ills of life those more awful ones of civil feud and bloody strife." Many Louisville Catholics were dismayed that Spalding did not reply to Prentice and his ilk in kind, but Spalding's irenic tone had good effect. The nativist politicians were themselves embarrassed over the riots, and tensions gradually eased. Within a year or so the Know-Nothings transferred their zeal to the slavery issue, and the Catholics breathed a collective sigh of relief. As has so often happened in the history of Christianity, the threats of persecution actually invigorated Catholic piety and cohesion. Attendance at Mass increased, and by the fall of 1856 Spalding could bask in the knowledge that the parochial schools were "as full as an egg—thanks to Know-Nothingism."

Though he did not shrink from defending his faith, Spalding's general approach to turmoil was spiritual. Hence the church in his view was not called upon to take political stands and was not a political threat. For the same reason Catholics did not associate themselves with controversial movements such as abolitionism. Because Spalding consistently took this position, the Catholic church was not destructively split by the Civil War which did so terribly divide and disrupt Kentucky. Hotheads might disagree with Spalding's low-keyed response to political causes, but the steady expansion of Kentucky Catholicism under his direction suggests the wisdom of his policy. A minority church with a sizable foreign constituency realistically had no other choice.

5

BLACK CHRISTIANITY

Historians are now beginning to understand the inner life of the slaves, the black community. Slaves clearly were not completely dehumanized by the brutalities of their existence. With a marvelous human resiliency they adapted to American realities, perhaps maintaining and adjusting some part of their African heritage, but primarily accommodating to the emergent white folk culture. The technical term for this complicated process of cultural accommodation is acculturation. In the total matrix of white-black relations in the antebellum South, no institution played a more significant role in acculturizing Africans to America than did the church.

Even in the earliest years of the seventeenth century, when the vast majority of slaves were "outlandish," or recently arrived from Africa, some attempts were made to Christianize them. At first owners hesitated because they feared Christian slaves might be declared legally free, but obliging laws soon made certain that conversion did not automatically lead to emancipation. Consequently there were numerous attempts to eradicate all traces of African background and teach slaves Christian precepts that were beneficial to the slaveowner: obedience and honesty became the prime tenets of the gospel taught by the masters. In the mid-eighteenth century, beginning with the evangelistic activities of the great Virginia divine, Samuel Davies, there awakened an interest in converting slaves. Devout masters and inspired revivalists were now often earnestly concerned about the state of the African's soul. While the practical benefits of religion as a method of social control were always important, the growing numbers of Baptist and Methodist preachers and laymen after the 1760s zealously spread their message with genuine solicitude for slaves as humans with souls precious in the sight of God. If converted slaves proved to be more obedient, that merely demonstrated the marvelous efficiency of God's word. Christian concern and racial regulation were welded into one.

The Baptists and Methodists, with their appeal to the poor, made the most black converts, although all the churches had slave members. Baptists and Methodists, at first mostly nonslaveowning whites, opposed slavery in their early days. Both had simple, soul-stirring, and emotional worship services replete with spirited singing, individual participation, and moving rituals like the Methodist love feasts and especially the Baptist baptismal exercises. It is conceivable that blacks could have remembered or been told of the existence of powerful river cults in Africa, and this might have made them especially susceptible to Baptist practice, but this could have had at most only marginal influence.

More likely the pietistic Christian denominations, with faiths that shaped their whole lives, were attractive to the slaves because their message and demeanor touched responsive chords of memory deep in the African past. Religion was, a Kenyan scholar has written, the "strongest element in [the African] traditional background, and exert[ed] probably the greatest influence upon the thinking and living of the people concerned." While most tribes believed in lesser nature gods and the ancestral spirits, practically all the African societies believed in a God who was the Supreme Being—omnipotent, omniscient, omnipresent. Moreover, most African peoples conceived God to be essentially good. This supreme God was seldom approached in traditional life; instead, the lesser gods and one's ancestors were appealed to as intermediaries. Yet in times of great distress, when deliverance or protection was sorely needed, the African peoples traditionally called upon God for comfort. This disposition to turn to God in a crisis, then, would probably have made slaves in the pathos of their American situation open to the Christian God proffered by the evangelicals. Religion in Africa suffused all life. Of course this pervasive religiosity also characterized the evangelicals, and thus the religious life-style they advocated was familiar and attractive to the African-born slaves.

One of the indispensable roles religion plays is to provide a sense of meaning and purpose for encountered dilemmas. In African traditional society, there were no irreligious persons. The land, village, ancestors, natural objects, all were molded by religious conceptions into a spiritualized environment. One's roots, security, and sense of existence were tied to this corporate religious society. The cultural shock experienced by the transplanted Africans was intensified precisely because removal put them out of contact with the nature gods and ancestral spirits to whom they normally appealed for support and survival. Since white owners often segregated slaves from their tribal groups, prohibited native languages, and systematically tried to extinguish any lingering remnants of African culture, imported blacks clearly suffered religious deprivation which was all the more shattering because of its cultural significance. While the African slaves maintained portions of their traditional religion, by a process of transference they came to accept the Christian God as the American counterpart of their traditional Supreme Being. But those far more numerous slaves born in America, removed from the African heritage and after about 1800 often surrounded by a pietistic Christian community, assimilated more completely the new religious culture. The result of this acculturation was a remarkably widespread and profound black Christianity in the South.

Historians have been slow to recognize the extent to which blacks and whites integrated religious activities in the antebellum South. Slave autobiographies and interviews often speak of whites reading the Bible to them on Sunday afternoons and of Sunday schools being established on the larger plantations and in the towns. A Kentuckian recorded in her diary, "A considerable interest on the subject of religion is manifest among the negroes, several have joined may they be kept by the power of God unto Salvation. The redemption of the soul is precious." This observation revealed a not atypical earnestness. In regions where there was a substantial black population, masters often built small chapels or "praise houses" where the blacks worshiped, usually in the presence of one or more whites, and developed surprising autonomy. In such areas as the densely black Sea Island district of South Carolina, black congregations prayed, preached, sang, and performed the "shout," a frenzied religious dance accompanied with music and emotions strikingly reminiscent of Africa. These exotic commotions have been vividly described, but they were far from representative of slave religion. Throughout most of the South in the nineteenth century, slave religion was much more conventional.

In the Bluegrass State slaves and master commonly came to church together and entered the same doorway. If the church had a gallery or balcony, the blacks worshiped there. In the absence of a balcony, the slaves sat at the rear of the church, where several pews were reserved for them. One slave remembered that in her local Methodist church, a gate separated the races. Whites and blacks heard the same sermons, mingled their appreciative "amens," sang the same hymns, took communion and were often baptized together, welcomed new members, and mutually underwent stringent church discipline. At

83

death they were buried in the same cemetery. Blacks constituted a sizable percentage of church membership throughout the antebellum South; in fact, they often outnumbered the whites in Baptist churches.

Even though there were black ministers who often preached with great effectiveness to mixed congregations and despite black deacons, elders, and association delegates, blacks were not accorded complete equality. Nevertheless, the degree of black participation was substantial. In an 1821 dispute that disrupted a Kentucky Baptist church, voting Negro members were decisive in settling the ministerial controversy. Forty years earlier black members of the Clear Creek Baptist Church had voted in the choice of a minister. Many white observers noted the depth and conviction of black Christians, and there are accounts of slaves traveling for miles to crowd into churches. It is hard to escape the conclusion that for such black believers, Christian faith was a central part of their culture. Even more emphatic are the stories of black Christians converting their owners.

There is perhaps no more arresting illustration of the extent to which blacks accommodated to the pietistic Protestantism of the Old South than that given by the extensive records on church discipline. The three dominant churches in Kentucky and in the South as a whole— Baptist, Methodist, and Presbyterian—had careful institutional machinery for watching over their members and correcting or punishing those who did wrong. Church discipline occupied an enormous amount of time and energy, but the result was a religious life that extended far beyond the formal sermons and actual church structures into every corner of personal life. A reading of the church records for any denomination reveals that slaves were accorded the same strict moral oversight. As with white members, slaves were called to account for drunkenness, profanity, inattendance at church, quarreling, adultery, and heresy. They were not held as rigidly accountable, but the difference was only a matter of degree.

Such mutual discipline says much about how whites viewed slaves, and how slaves viewed themselves. Slaves were very seldom forced to attend the white-dominated church. They voluntarily came and submitted to strict codes of behavior. Slaves were not fawning, servile Christians; rather they participated actively in the church courts, bearing testimony not only about the moral failings of fellow slaves but also—at least on some occasions—of ruthless slaveowners. Blacks in bondage were expected to conform spiritually to the same codes as whites. That they were frequently upbraided for adultery, like white transgressors, shows that slave marriage was expected even if it was extralegal. Indeed, Christianity was a main prop supporting the black family in a legal situation that denied it legitimacy. Whites and blacks found religious as well as economic and psychological justification for the sanctity of slave marriages and stable families, and owners were hesitant to transgress the moral code in the absence of dire economic pressure. The slave trade, miscegenation, and black promiscuity were restrained by the pietistic principles of southern society. Slavery paradoxically was an immoral socioeconomic institution moderated by moral constraints. In general, a wide reading of church and synod minutes illustrates a remarkable community of religious beliefs, one that included both races under the sacred canopy of evangelical Protestantism. All conformed to identical moral expectations, perhaps the only place in southern society where bond and free so nearly met as equals. It is no wonder slaves found church participation meaningful, for it bestowed upon them their safest symbol of self-respect and provided a public arena for moral growth and self-improvement.

Precisely because religion offered to the slave the clearest glimpse of his own worth and made manifest the value of striving to overcome the temptations and frustrations of this world, it was potentially subversive of the institution of slavery. Whites and blacks recognized this, and much of the dynamics of southern worship reflected their awareness. White religious leaders therefore took pains to control both the times of black worship and the actual theology preached. Whites and blacks worshiping together developed naturally as a matter of convenience, but quickly biracial services were deemed obligatory as a means of controlling who presented the gospel to the slaves. No white clergyman wanted a separate, independent black church to form. They feared the rebellious implications of such a development and earnestly felt that black ignorance, superstition, and romantic emotionalism would soon corrupt the tenets of white Christianity. The Reverend C. C. Jones, for example, in his manual to whites on how to instruct slaves in religion, argued that biracial services tend "to increase subordination." If blacks were kept dependent upon whites for their religious sustenance, no true black leaders would develop.

This concern did not prevent special services for the black members on Sunday afternoons or other specified times, but the white minister conducted the services. If the black members were numerous enough to crowd the church, then an adjunct black church would be constructed, but its subordination to the sister white body was explicit. The Baptist church at Stamping Ground, Kentucky, had such a large black membership that in October 1840 several Negroes were appointed to oversee any disorder that might arise. This seems to have accentuated a feeling of separateness among the slaves, for following this date they held separate meetings, "prayed, preached, and exhorted" at their own services, received members and exercised strict discipline, all the while presided over by the white moderator and clerk of the church. Despite this superintendence, black religious autonomy and black consciousness grew. By 1850 blacks were raising money to build a separate house of worship, and by 1855 they had successfully completed a comfortable structure. Then the Baptist church at Stamping Ground appointed a committee to study the question of

86

forming a separate black church under its supervision. The committee reluctantly recognized that slaves increasingly preferred their own black-directed services. Consequently in February 1855 the African Baptist church at Stamping Ground was officially organized with all-black leadership (though still under the supervision of the white committee), and it accepted the "covenant, creed and rules of decorum" of the mother church. With their black preachers and substantial independence, the church prospered, reporting 335 members in 1859.

Although most black congregations did not become separate and fully independent until after 1865, the scattered African branches of white churches played a significant role in the black community. Slaves practiced a degree of self-government, they developed black leaders and their own religious expertise, and they learned to depend upon themselves for spiritual improvement. Such avenues for leadership development and the creation of black religious communities vastly expanded the psychic living space of slaves. Black Christian faith succeeded in part in preventing the institution of slavery from becoming the psychologically crippling system it might have been otherwise.

The white clergy were not content simply to monitor the physical setting of worship services for slaves; they also attempted to circumscribe the actual theology preached and heard. Scripture often speaks of the value of persons, of doing unto others as one would be done unto, of being freed from the slavery of sin, of knowing the truth and thereby being set free. From the slaveowner's perspective, the Bible must be interpreted narrowly, literally, and legally to avoid its subversive implications. However, this literalism was not peculiar to race relations; it was the general mode of scriptural interpretation in the antebellum South. Slaveowners and cooperative clergy also sought to make Christianity practical and supportive of the peculiar institution.

The first generation of ministers—approximately until

87

1800—often expressed antislavery sentiments. Then following the abortive Gabriel Revolt of 1800 in Virginia and culminating with Nat Turner's insurrection in 1831, white ministers became increasingly cautious. Over and over the slave narratives tell of white preachers minimizing the grander themes of salvation, justification, and regeneration and instead pronouncing with mechanical regularity the importance of obeying their masters. Even those white clergy morally committed to saving the souls of blacks, those who rose above social control to preach the joy of faith, nevertheless found themselves pressed to censor their sermons to support the status quo.

Blacks were allowed secondary leadership roles by the white religious institutions. The most important of these roles was that of the local black preacher, probably the most significant position open to slaves. No doubt many black preachers hewed to the self-serving gospel prescribed by the whites, but most, especially when beyond the hearing of white supervisors, contributed to the development of a distinct black Christianity. Slave marriages and deaths were often solemnized by slave ministers. The black preacher was a common figure in antebellum Kentucky. Even the famous Traveling Church included among its members a black preacher, Uncle Peter. He subsequently purchased his freedom and that of his wife, moved to Lexington, and established the thriving First African Baptist Church. At his death the church had some three hundred members. Later there were black ministers in the Baptist, Disciples of Christ, Methodist, and Presbyterian churches and black lay leaders renowned for their piety in the Catholic and Episcopal churches.

There are several indications that the institution of slavery was less harsh in Kentucky than in other southern states. The Reverend Josiah Henson, the famous prototype for Harriet Beecher Stowe's Uncle Tom, recorded in his autobiography that upon being moved from Maryland to the Bluegrass State in 1825, he found that "In Kentucky, the opportunities of attending the preaching of whites, as well as of blacks, were more numerous; and partly by attending them, and the camp-meetings which occurred from time to time, and partly from studying carefully my own heart," Henson decided to begin preaching. He soon was authorized to preach by the Quarterly Conference of the Methodist Episcopal church, since "no great amount of theological knowledge" was necessary for one to become a local Methodist minister. As another slave preacher remarked, "I am no mathematician, no biologist, neither grammarian, but when it comes to handling the Bible I knocks down verbs, breaks up prepositions and jumps over adjectives . . . I am a God sent man."

Black preachers were clearly natural leaders, men of substantial ability, forceful personality, and possessors of what we might today call stage presence. They were figures of real importance to their black communities, the one-of-their-own whom slaves looked up to for guidance and leadership. One example will illustrate this relationship. The Reverend Lewis Craig, who died in 1847, had owned the Reverend George DuPuy, black minister of the Pleasant Green Baptist Church in Lexington. When Craig's will was finally probated, his property, including George DuPuy, was listed for sale. DuPuy's loyal and distraught congregation importuned the minister of the sister white church to help them purchase their preacher's freedom. The white deacons agreed to buy DuPuy for the black congregation and allow them to reimburse the cost on an installment basis. The deal was struck, and even though DuPuy brought $830, the black congregation had saved their minister from the slave trade; each Monday they made a small repayment to the white church. Such sacrificial loyalty indicates the bond between black preachers and their flock.

As the foregoing suggests, black ministers were allowed special but limited privileges within the slave society. There are examples of black exhorters being given permission to preach even where there were no whites and to travel unmolested. Such freedom was minimal, but it was unusual for blacks in the antebellum South. In 1856 one minister in Kentucky was given the following pass: "Tom is my slave, and has permission to go to Louisville for two or three weeks and return after he has made his visit. Tom is a preacher of the reformed Baptist Church, and has always been a faithful servant." A young slave named Daniel, who in 1818 said he wished "to exercise a publick gift" of preaching, was authorized by his white church to "exercise his gift" at stated times, although whites had to be present. Later he was given permission to preach in the white meetinghouse to both races on the first and third Sundays of the month, unless a white minister was present. Soon he was allowed to preach to his own race at any time when no white minister was available, but he was prevented from holding night meetings. The eminent London Ferrill, a free black minister, made the First African Baptist Church in Lexington, with 1,820 members in 1854, the largest church in Kentucky. It was an independent black church, having no affiliation with any white church that supervised its activities.

Ferrill's church was not unique. In addition to black churches adjunct to parent white churches, on the eve of the Civil War there were in Kentucky seventeen independent black Baptist churches, having an aggregate membership of 5,737. Many of these members were probably free Negroes, but a substantial number were slaves. There were black churches of other denominations as well—Louisville had a total of nine African churches in 1860. Sir Charles Lyell, the geologist, visited a black Methodist church there in 1846 which had a congregation of 400 in a large, gas-lit building. Perhaps because of the inhibiting presence of the distinguished visitor, the sermon was only occasionally punctuated with "amens" and other heartfelt signs of approval. According to Lyell, the "preacher was a full black, spoke good English, and quoted Scripture well." And in a rather abstract discourse, he "spoke of our ancestors in the garden of Eden in a manner that left no doubt of his agreeing . . . that we all came from one pair."

Lyell did not develop this point, but the minister's apparent argument is significant: if both whites and blacks are descendants from a common ancestor, then all are brothers and equal in the eyes of God. The unspoken extension of this idea is that slavery is biologically and morally wrong. Lyell had obviously encountered a bold and learned black minister—white Methodist sermons certainly did not deal as a rule with such abstractions. Lyell himself noted that the service was more orderly and dignified than that of a white Methodist church he had visited in Montgomery, Alabama. Probably more typical of black worship was that described in the mid-1850s by a New England visitor to a Louisville African church: "The meeting commences with singing, through the whole congregation. Louder and louder still were their devotions—and oh! what music, what devotion, what streaming eyes, and throbbing hearts; my blood ran quick in my veins, and quicker still. . . . It seems as though the roof would rise from the walls, and some of them would go up, soul and body both."

Although there were stereotyped figures, like the minister Peter Cotton who had scriptural texts embroidered on his coat so he literally could be clothed in righteousness, no one better illustrates the opportunities and restrictions of the slave preacher than the Reverend Elisha Green of Maysville, Kentucky. As a child in Bourbon County in the 1820s, Green attended surreptitious black religious meetings, once barely escaping the patrollers who arrived to disrupt the service. Sometimes the night services were protected by taut grapevines stretched across the roads, which would knock the mounted patrollers to the ground. Such sermons as Green heard were instrumental in his conversion, which occurred several years later while he was plowing in Mason County.

91

Shortly afterwards he was baptized. About this time he was hired to work in a store in Maysville. He learned simple mathematics by having to weigh and count goods in the store, and the storeowner's young daughter taught him to read.

Simultaneously for years he was sexton of the Maysville Baptist Church, hearing many sermons as he worshiped with the whites. Eventually Green was moved to do "something for God." Recognizing his abilities, several white deacons obtained permission from Green's owner, the storekeeper, to license Green to preach. Thus the Maysville Baptist Church on May 10, 1845, unanimously "*Resolved,* That Elisha Green, the property of John P. Dobbyns of this city, has full liberty and permission from this day to exercise his gifts in the public before the colored population of this city or any others before whom in the providence of God he may be cast." Subsequently Green was ordained.

From that time forward Green preached widely throughout northern and central Kentucky, sometimes being opposed but always finding white support. Soon he was minister of the African Baptist church at Paris, where the blacks had formed their own church. The rules for the black church clearly made it subject to the supervision of the whites, and legally the African church was subservient to the white church. But even within that limited sphere, slave members probably found the greatest amount of freedom and autonomy possible in a slave culture. One suspects the white supervision over the everyday life of the church was minimal, allowing Green and his slave congregation even greater freedom to carve a cultural enclave out of their world of bondage.

Yet there was still another dimension to the religious life of slaves, one further removed from both the white churches and the adjunct black churches with black ministers. Despite or because of their relative freedom to develop a religious subculture of their own in scattered African churches and to worship and participate in white religious services throughout the region, slaves ultimately found their religious needs unfulfilled by such a secondhand faith. In secret religious meetings held at night in urban hideaways, slave cabins, or in secluded forest clearings, where they were free from white supervision, free to worship as they pleased, and free to sing their spirituals, slaves developed a distinct black Christian culture whose influence is still felt today in black churches. This faith, with possibly an admixture of vague Africanisms, was a genuine black folk religion that ministered to slaves in their peculiar unfree status in the land of the free. In it slaves found a modicum of freedom, the more treasured and powerful because it was their own creation.

Repeatedly slaves in their autobiographies and interviews tell of their efforts to escape the religious supervision of the whites. When, for example, the tolling each night at 10 o'clock of the bell on the Fourth Street Presbyterian Church in Louisville signaled that all slaves had to be home and accounted for, on pain of receiving fifteen lashes and being jailed the rest of the night, the white church must have symbolized degrading repressment at least as much as genuine solicitude for the slaves' eternal souls. Slaves often learned only the barest rudiments of the Christian gospel from the white minister and the black preachers speaking under the watchful eye of whites. As one ex-slave recalled, "The biggest thing I heard them preach about was, 'Servants, obey your mistress and master.' They would tell them not to steal. *Very few of them told you about religion.*" Having heard primarily a self-serving echo of the Christian message addressed to them from ministers in formal settings, slaves desired to hear the heart of the gospel: themes of love, salvation, regeneration, and heaven. As a result, slaves throughout the region conspired to meet secretly so, independent of the cramping supervision of whites, they could discover the hope and ecstasy of pietistic Protestantism. This was precisely what whites did not

93

want—blacks developing strong leaders, organizational skills, and a possible religious rationale for rebellion. But the underground black religious services thrived nevertheless.

Often on Sunday evenings slaves slipped away to appointed meetings. In every region they often used one curious technique which they believed would guarantee the secrecy of their worship. Whenever they met indoors, they would turn upside down on the floor a kettle, cooking pot, or wash pot to "catch" the sound of their singing and praising. Sometimes the pot would be placed in the center of the floor, at other times near the door; usually it was slightly tipped on one edge to allow the sound to rush under. This device was used throughout the South, and its origin is unclear. But believing themselves safe in the depths of forests or protected by the pot from roaming white patrollers, slaves in these secret services developed their own form of Christian worship and their own theological emphases. Their leader was usually a slave who either could read the Bible or had learned substantial portions of it from public church services or a pious owner. Numerous masters and mistresses read the Scriptures to their slaves, and obviously since blacks attended most white churches, they had to hear many sermons or substantial portions of many sermons which elaborated the full gospel. The black Christianity that emerged was remarkably biblical, though refracted through the life experience of the slaves.

The Old Testament God and the New Testament Jesus are similar in many ways; both are revealed to be remarkably involved with people. Black Christians strongly emphasized a personal relationship between the divine and the believer. God and Jesus could be one's intimate friends, helpmates in times of trouble. Jesus in the role of the Suffering Servant was most attractive to slaves. The Old Testament story of God's chosen people who were enslaved, brutally mistreated, dispersed, and yet ultimately under the protection and guidance of the Almighty was also extremely attractive to slaves, who closely identified their plight with that of the ancient Hebrews. In Jesus slaves found a personal deliverer and in their self-identification with the epic of the Hebrews they discovered self-respect and moral superiority. So even though there was a powerful Christological emphasis within black Christianity, it simultaneously nurtured moving Old Testament analogies. A judging God and a personal savior were equal parts of the slave theology. The rare rebels like Nat Turner and the many long-suffering blacks of the type William Faulkner has portrayed were both legitimate heirs of slave Christianity.

From the Old Testament lessons, slaves accepted God's rule over the world and man's essential sinfulness; from their New Testament belief in a personal savior came their faith in Jesus Christ. They maintained the paradox of an omnipotent and omniscient God awesomely mighty and filled with splendor, and a world filled with sin, tragedy, inhumanity, slavery, and death. They recognized their world was the same as Abraham's. Yet Jesus was sent by God as a means of overcoming the world, and many slaves profoundly realized the reconciliation and freedom offered by the New Testament Jesus. In the person of Jesus they found forgiveness in the sight of God, and this miracle brought them not only awe but even more important, self-respect and hope. Forgiven, they were at one with God and thus impervious ultimately to the trials of this world. One slave preacher, being painfully whipped by slave patrollers, said as the blows fell, "Jesus Christ suffered for righteousness' sake, so kin I." Forgiven and reconciled with God, they believed themselves morally and spiritually superior to their white masters. As Frederick Douglass remarked, "Slaveholders may sometimes have confidence in the piety of some of their slaves, but slaves seldom have confidence in the piety of their masters." The image of God's chosen people Israel as suffering but still chosen and the role of Jesus as the man who suffered for others enabled slaves in the midst of physical cruelty and a chattel bondage that legally deprived them of personhood to discover a measure of self-worth and spiritual strength capable of giving meaning and value to life. Here was the sustenance that enabled the black personality to prevail despite two centuries of slavery.

Life was to be accepted, not rebelled against in some sort of self-destructive rage. Forgiveness meant being able to accept oneself while outwardly acquiescing to the institution of slavery. Forgiveness provided the strength of character to endure slavery without being enslaved psychologically. Here was a type of submission that because of its religious nature paradoxically made the slave the spiritual victor over his master. Here was a profound spiritual rebellion that while it subdued hate and feelings of personal worthlessness, spared the rebel from the almost certain death physical insurrection would bring. Christianity gave blacks a superb perseverance, one that invigorated ethical earnestness and looked forward to an eschatological judgment day. In the end times, a just God would recompense the long-suffering slave Christians. This vivid and complete trust in a glorious heaven was looked forward to as a deserved reward and a final proof of the spiritual superiority of the despised and downtrodden slave. Correspondingly, slaveholders would get their just rewards in hell.

The best-known aspect of slave Christianity was the black spirituals, those haunting melodies which still have the power to move congregations. Spirituals represent a unique contribution to American culture, incorporating African rhythms and tonal patterns with evangelical Protestantism. The vocabulary and stories are biblical—Moses, Ole Pharaoh, Joshua, Jesus—and the sentiment is both Christian and human: the life experience of the slaves made its impress on every spiritual. Song was as much a part of the slaves' life as sadness and suffering, and singing was a universal mode of expression. As an aged ex-slave remarked, "colored folks . . . certainly got the harp in their mouths." The words to spirituals were seldom written; individual songs were constantly subject to improvisation, evolution, and particularization. A remarkable event, a new birth, a sudden storm would be incorporated into songs, with the entire group suggesting and approving the lyrical innovations made by a leader. Spirituals were community efforts, speaking of otherworldly ideals and this world's realities. They were first and foremost religious songs, portraying God's way for a suffering people who would persist and triumph ultimately in heaven. In one sense they were otherworldly, but in a more accurate sense they ministered to the heartfelt needs of a people who shouldered the heavy burdens of this world.

The themes of black spirituals paralleled those of black theology. Many spoke of the Old Testament God who watched over his people, the enslaved Hebrews, and eventually delivered them from their slavery. He was a God who punished his enemies—"Joshua Fit de Battle of Jericho"—who gave rest to the heavy laden—"Mos' Done Toilin' Here"—who rescued his people from bondage—"Go Down, Moses." In addition to this black identification with the Children of Israel, there were strong New Testament emphases: songs of joy about the baby Jesus, songs of sorrow about the crucifixion, and many songs about heaven, where there was freedom from the sorrows of this world, families were united, justice was observed. Because of this longing for Judgment Day and heaven, many spirituals (and black sermons) have a pronounced apocalyptic tone. But these were primarily sacred songs, not subtle calls for insurrection. Again they offered slaves a feeling of moral superiority through equating themselves with the Children of Israel; slaves via spirituals could identify themselves with God's plan that those who suffered unjustly would eventually be rewarded.

Some commentators have described slave religion as a

"home base for revolution" and seen every secret religious meeting as a plotting session for rebellion, every lyric of "steal away, steal away to Jesus" as a call to escape to the North. There is no denying that there were religious motivations or at least rhetoric behind the Gabriel, Denmark Vesey, and Nat Turner revolts, but these events, though based on a rationale compatible with the Old Testament emphasis of black Christianity, seem most atypical.

It has become fashionable to argue that black religion was inherently radical in a secular sense, that its practitioners were preaching this-worldly militance under the guise of religious terminology. Frederick Douglass's apt comment is often quoted: "A keen observer might have detected in our repeated singing of 'O Canaan, sweet Canaan,/I am bound for the land of Canaan,' something more than a hope of reaching heaven. We meant to reach the *North*, and the North was our Canaan." But Douglass makes clear that he and his coconspirators had already made the momentous decision to escape. Few slaves ever seriously planned to escape to the North, few rebelled as openly and forthrightly as Douglass. He himself admitted that his actions "distinguished me among my servile brethren." For most slaves, rebellion was internalized. Thus while to Douglass, having plunged into a plot to flee to freedom, the spiritual refrain "Run to Jesus, shun the danger./I don't expect to stay/Much longer here," meant "a speedy pilgrimage to a free state," he also recognized that "on the lips of some it meant the expectation of a speedy summons to a world of spirits."

The submission to bondage was, in many instances, merely a conscious way of coping with the exigencies of life in a slave society. Submission was not total but controlled; it reflected the limited possibilities for overt action and the kind of sublimated moral rebellion permissible. For the huge majority of slaves, their folk Christianity provided them both a spiritual release and a spiritual victory. They could inwardly repudiate the system and thus steel themselves to survive it. This more subtle, more profound type of spiritual freedom made their Christianity the most significant aspect of slave culture and effectively defused the potential for insurrection. Repeatedly the narratives tell of slaves having their souls "freed." One aged ex-slave even remarked that she often heard her mother say, " 'I am so glad I am free.' I did not know then what she was talking about. I thought she meant freedom from slavery." It was precisely this belief that one was in the ultimate sense "free" that allowed countless slaves to persevere so eloquently. In ways masters never suspected, black Christianity prevented slave uprisings.

Another exaggerated segment of slave culture has been the role of superstition and "trick doctors" or conjurers. Some have emphasized these as Africanisms, strange rites and beliefs that were wedded to Christian doctrines to produce a syncretistic black Christianity. There were few conjurers, and their influence was largely confined to the largest, most isolated plantations in limited portions of the South before the end of the slave trade in 1808. Some Africanisms no doubt survived, perhaps most vividly in the music of the spirituals and such customs as the turned-up pot used to muffle sounds. Possibly the attraction of the personal emphasis of the Baptists and Methodists was related to tribal beliefs in individualized spirits. But most of the superstitions held by slaves—ghosts, haunted houses, the "signs," evil spirits, witches—were also common to Anglo-Saxon culture. Rural, uneducated whites and blacks probably shared such superstitions. To label most slave superstitions tenacious Africanisms then seems to be stretching analysis.

In summary, religion was an integral part of black culture in antebellum Kentucky. By identifying themselves with the Children of Israel, whom God eventually delivered from their enemies, and by grasping Jesus as their savior and the exemplar of the Suffering Servant, many slaves discovered the inner strength to survive chattel slavery and keep their personalities remarkably intact. The black family, the black psyche, the black will to endure until someday when they would overcome their servitude, all owe much to the strength of the slaves' Christian faith. Their belief held them together as a people, gave joy and hope to a world filled with sorrow and sadness, and offered a subtle and devastating critique of slavery without requiring self-destructive insurrection. Without their religion, slaves would likely have found their existence unendurable, resulting in genocidal race war and destructive self-hate. The peculiar institution was a frightfully evil system; but except for black Christianity it might have had even more injurious issue for the consequent history of race relations in this state and nation.

6

WHITE CHURCHES
AND BLACK SLAVERY

IN THE YEARS before the Civil War cut through the nation like an avenging sword and excised the cancerous evil of slavery, Kentuckians prided themselves on the mild features of bondage in their state. There were comparatively fewer slaves in Kentucky than in most other southern states, and there were fewer absentee owners. With the Ohio River as a border offering freedom across her banks, the real possibility of escape via the underground railroad forced many Kentucky slaveowners to ameliorate the kind of abuses that existed in the Deep South. The mountainous terrain in the east, the river cities like Louisville (and Cincinnati across the river) in which slaves could find varied occupations and blend in with the free blacks, the prevalence of small farmers in the southern counties, all contributed to Kentucky's avoiding the kind of dictatorial slave regime that often characterized other sections. The result was a surprising tradition of antislavery led by the churches. And unlike most emancipatory movements, the Kentucky societies were not led by Quakers. This heritage was begun in 1792 by David Rice and continued for six stormy decades. For the open intensity of its emancipatory tradition, Kentucky stands like a beacon among the southern states. Yet it was a clouded beacon, for moral commitment by the few, and courage aplenty, could not erase the majority's rival commitment to slavery.

Slavery had a corrosive quality on the entire southern experience, eating away at the values that once promised to stand at the center of southern civilization. Freedom of thought, libertarian views, the republic of the yeoman farmer, all fell beneath the onrush of the slavery-plantation regime. The South, once the liberal center of the nation, became its conservative backwater. Freedom of expression, when it touched the region's peculiar institution, was largely curtailed after the 1830s. The aristocratic values of the slaveocracy came to dominate what might otherwise have been the land of the plain folk, for slavery was much more than an arrangement of labor relations. It became a social system, ordering all other human relations. The possession of slaves became a badge of personal merit. Every reform plan, every scheme for change had to be considered in the shadow of slavery. With slavery so firmly entrenched, the inability of reformers to effect emancipation is not surprising. What is unexpected is the existence of a religious tradition of abolitionism in Kentucky. Yet, ironically and tragically, this movement was doomed from the beginning, for it never became more than a minority's commitment, and the theology of southern evangelicalism was one that ultimately disclaimed societal responsibility. As a result the churches in general supported the status quo, and slavery was thus not ended in Kentucky before the Civil War.

David Rice's opposition to slavery was widely known before he was elected to the convention that wrote Kentucky's first state constitution in 1792. Three months before the convention met in May, he had published *Slavery Inconsistent with Justice and Good Policy,* the first antislavery publication west of the Appalachians. As Rice, tall, slender, and dignified, gave his earnest oration before the assembled delegates, many were doubtlessly moved by the logic and passion of his words. Nevertheless, slaveholders dominated the convention, and the infamous Article IX passed, placing Kentucky's slavery on a firm legal foundation. Rice's pamphlet and speech, however, did articulate the views of others of several faiths, and his influence led Kentucky Presbyterians to sustain a moderate emancipatory stance for several years before pressure from the slaveholding society forced a fateful retreat from principle.

The thesis of Rice's pamphlet was that slavery was morally and practically wrong because it was contrary both to justice and to sound policy. He argued that the slave was "a rational creature reduced by the power of legislation to the state of a brute, and thereby deprived of every privilege of humanity." If this were not enough to convince fence-straddlers of the evil of slavery, Rice went on to describe the crimes perpetrated against slaves, showing how they were the helpless victims of sexual outrages, beatings, and so on. Then he turned to his practical arguments, asking whether it was "good policy to keep a numerous, a growing body of people among us, who add no strength to us in time of war; who are under the strongest temptations to join an enemy, . . . who will count so many against us in an hour of danger and distress." And he made clear that slaves had absolutely no reason to trust and defend those who daily betrayed their most sacred rights. In fact, slavery was "a standing monument of the tyranny and inconsistency of human governments." Such inconsistency between national principles and local practice harmed American prestige abroad and undermined domestic confidence.

Though in his listing of the evils of slavery Rice advocated the rights of blacks, a substantial portion of his attack on slavery was grounded in his belief that it harmed the white society. "Slavery naturally tends to sap the foundations of moral, and consequently of political virtue," he wrote, "and virtue is absolutely necessary for the happiness and prosperity of a free people. Slavery produces idleness; and idleness is the nurse of vice." Such idleness also lessened "national prosperity." In addition, the habit of control to which the master is addicted "puffs up the mind with pride" and "tends to destroy all sense of justice and equity." Slavery was manifestly inconsistent with good policy.

Some might argue, Rice admitted, that general emancipation would lead to miscegenation and an eventual mongrelization of the white race. But candor should lead us to admit, he wrote, "that it is too late to prevent this great imaginary evil; the matter is already gone beyond recovery; for it may be proved, with mathematical certainty, that if things go on in the present channel, the future inhabitants of America will inevitably be Mulattoes." Rice no doubt exaggerated the amount of miscegenation, but by so doing he deftly lanced the smug hypocrisy of those who opposed emancipation because they feared such an act would lead to barbarous genetic consequences. And for those who fell back upon a biblical defense of slavery, Rice devoted five pages to a concise refutation of such a reading of the Bible which so brazenly violated the great principle of the golden rule. Rising to the magnitude of the moment, Rice eloquently concluded that the convention should "resolve unconditionally to put an end to slavery in Kentucky." Yet this great performance, at the crucial beginning of statehood when the liberal principles of the Revolution were yet alive, failed. Slavery, despite the tradition of opposition so nobly propounded by Rice, was to dominate the society and churches even of Kentucky. Such was the measure of the tragedy.

Rice's impassioned speech in 1792 was but the beginning of Presbyterian efforts to end slavery in Kentucky. Yet the conservative, gradualist nature of their program must be emphasized. Like many others living in the warm afterglow of the Revolution's liberalism, the Presbyterians honestly believed slavery was a dying institution. They aimed both to ameliorate the slaves' condition now and to prepare them for their eventual life of freedom. It was in this context that the Transylvania Presbytery in 1794 ordered that slaveholders "shall teach every slave not above the age of fifteen years to read the word of God and give them such education as may prepare them for the enjoyment of freedom, and shall instruct such slaves of the above description, and all others under their care, as far as they can find it practicable in the principles and precepts of the Christian religion." The following year, the Transylvania Presbytery sent to the General Assembly, their national body, queries regarding the propriety of emancipationists' remaining in fellowship with slaveholders. The General Assembly, fearing disruption of the denomination, urged a spirit of forbearance. It warned of "differences of opinion" that "threatened divisions which may have the most ruinous tendency." Certainly a formal if implicit condemnation of slaveholders would have destroyed the denomination in Kentucky. (It was exactly such forbearance that prevented Rice and his coemancipationists from founding an antislavery society in the mid-1790s. They hoped a convention would be called shortly to consider revising the 1792 constitution, and they reasoned "that prior to this it would not be prudent to give such an alarm to the slaveholders . . . the friends of equal liberty, by making a premature exertion, might lose their influence in the election of a future Convention." So to avoid contention, antislavery was soft-pedaled in church and politics.) The General Assembly appointed Rice to a committee to draft a recommendation on slavery, and although this document was rejected by the assembly for the less controversial appeal for coexistence between slaveholders and emancipationists, the conservative nature of the proposed document is striking. It conceded that "Freedom is desirable, but cannot at all times be enjoyed with advantage. . . . A slave let loose upon society ignorant, idle, and headstrong, is in a state to injure others and ruin himself. . . . The slave must first be in a situation to act properly as a member of civil society before he can be advantageously introduced therein." The General Assembly then referred the presbytery to its previous recommendation that slaves be taught to read and thus prepared for freedom.

By 1796 Kentucky Presbyterians had made the fatal compromise which throughout the South emasculated religious abolitionism. Petitions and queries having again been brought to it, the Transylvania Presbytery, pressured from above by the General Assembly and more immediately pressured from below by local public opinion, adopted the following resolution:

That although the Presbytery are fully convinced of the great evil of slavery; yet they view the final remedy as alone belonging to the civil powers; and also do not think that they have sufficient authority from the word of God to make it a term of church communion. They, therefore, leave it to the conscience of the brethren to act as they may think proper; earnestly recommending to the people under their care to emancipate such of their slaves as they may think fit subjects of liberty; and that they also take every possible measure, by teaching their young slaves to read and giving them such other instruction as may be in their power, to prepare them for the enjoyment of liberty, an event which they contemplate with the greatest pleasure, and which they hope, will be accomplished as soon as the nature of things will admit.

By abdicating ultimate responsibility to the civil government, by leaving the moral issue to individual conscience, and by refusing to make emancipation a matter of discipline or communion, the Presbyterians were left with an emancipatory policy in the abstract and a de facto defense of the status quo. The next year the presbytery, in response to queries, determined that slavery was a moral evil but that slaveholders were not guilty of moral evil. When the logic of such an apparent paradox was questioned, the churchmen resolved "that the question now before presbytery is of so much importance that the consideration of it be put off till a future day." They never answered the query; a moral issue had again been sacrificed to local considerations. Thereafter Kentucky Presbyterians worked to educate slaves and improve their conditions; they occasionally disciplined a master who whipped his slaves to excess or sold one who was a church member. Despite their early intentions, the church gradually became a strong defender of the surrounding society, developing no critique of societal ills. Individual lapses such as drunkenness were condemned, but the church felt no larger community responsibility. In a slave society reform was limited by the recognition of reality. Ironically David Rice indicated the depth of the problem in a letter to a prominent member of the Pennsylvania Society for the Abolition of Slavery: "I find but few, who will undertake to justify slavery, or defend it on moral principles; but many, who endeavour to excuse themselves, lay the blame on others, and on the difficulties attending the emancipation of slaves. Interest, all powerful Interest, closes the eyes and hardens the heart to a great degree: it gives the least plausible pretense the force of the strongest arguments." Even Rice himself, fearful of what might happen to his slaves if they were emancipated in a racist world, never did so, and at his death in 1816 willed them to his daughter.

Perhaps the corrosive effects of slavery upon principle is nowhere more tragically illustrated than within the Methodist church. In its formative years the Methodist church was composed primarily of the poorer sort who owned no slaves and were in general critical of the materialistic values of the planter class. Taking their cue from John Wesley and led by British-born evangelists like Francis Asbury, the infant Methodist sect professed firm abolitionist views. At their annual conference in 1780 they acknowledged that slavery was "contrary to the laws of God, man, and nature, and hurtful to society, contrary to the dictates of conscience and pure religion, and doing that which we would not others do to us and ours," and therefore voted their "disapprobation" of those who owned slaves. When four years later at the famous Christmas Conference in Baltimore the Methodist Episcopal church was formally organized, a slavery clause was written into the new church's *Discipline*. At this conference there were no representatives from Virginia (home of half of America's Methodists), and the meeting was dominated by the ideas of Wesley and his specially chosen representative, Thomas Coke, a fiery emancipationist. Coke with the prestige of John Wesley behind him pushed through a statement on slavery far stronger than native American Methodists would have independently accepted.

This new rule began by stating that slavery was "contrary to the golden law of God on which hang all the law and the prophets, and the unalienable rights of mankind, as well as every principle of the revolution." Consequently every Methodist layman who owned slaves was required to free them within a stated number of years on pain of being excluded from membership and communion. Methodist ministers had previously been required to free their slaves, but few of them had owned any. Now the rule extended to all members, and this was the crux of the Methodist dilemma. Laymen in the South who owned slaves and were members of a local Methodist society were loathe to free their slaves no matter what the *Discipline* might say. The delegates at the Christmas Conference tacitly understood this reality, for the *Discipline* went on to say, "These rules are to affect the members of our society no farther than is consistent with the laws of the states in which they reside." Moreover, Virginians were given a two-year period of grace wherein they could "consider the expedience of compliance or non-compliance with these rules." Thus even in the *Discipline*'s most forthright stand against slavery, there was built in an avenue for moral retreat.

In fact in 1784 only North Carolina prohibited manumission, but opposition to emancipation was strong in

Virginia. In early 1785 Coke traveled through Virginia to test the Methodists' sentiments, and he was astounded at their resistance. At the June 1785 conference the offending rules were suspended. Nevertheless, the Methodist church continued to oppose slavery in the abstract, stating: "We do hold in the deepest abhorrence, the practice of slavery; and shall not cease to seek its destruction by all wise and prudent means." But the exigencies of southern life closely constricted what might be termed prudence.

Had Methodism been willing to remain a tiny, sectlike group alienated from the larger society, it might have been able to maintain its early antislavery position. Speaking from a close-knit spiritual community that had no aspirations to growth, the Methodists, like the Quakers, might have served as the antislavery conscience of the South. But race relations did not loom as large in the world view of eighteenth-century Methodists as it does in ours. They felt their primary mission was to spread the gospel message to all God's creatures and rightly recognized that to be labeled as abolitionists would deprive them of most evangelistic opportunities in the South. Not only would slaveowners restrict Methodist access to the slaves but also the slaveowners would close their own ears and hearts to a message that threatened the precarious institution of slavery. Faced with the choice of remaining insignificantly few in numbers if they were morally uncompromising, or possibly evangelizing the entire South, black and white, if they would but make "prudent" concessions to the region's racial demands, the Methodists made a conscious choice. They did not abandon their opposition to slavery—many individual ministers and laymen continued outspoken—but they played down their disciplinary restrictions.

This compromise to southern conditions emerged in the decade after 1785. Beginning in 1796 the *Discipline*'s rules against slaveholding were progressively weakened. That year the requirement that ministers free or arrange to free their slaves in the near future was modified to include the statement "as the laws of the state respectively, and the circumstances of the case will admit." It took little imagination in the slaveholding regions to discover "circumstances" that suggested compromise. The General Conference of 1796 also allowed regional and state yearly conferences "to make whatever regulations they judge proper . . . respecting the admission of persons to official stations" in the church. Moreover, rather than require all would-be members who owned slaves to free their slaves in order to become a Methodist, the 1796 *Discipline* merely required that "no slaveholder shall be received into society, till the preacher who has oversight of the circuit, has spoken to him freely and faithfully on the subject of slavery." Even though the conference strongly ruled against the slave trade and made clear its opposition to slavery, institutional accommodation to slavery had already penetrated the church. That the 1800 General Conference required local conferences to "draw up addresses for the gradual emancipation of the slaves" and send them to their state legislatures did not change the crucial compromise of purity to expansion. In 1804 the General Conference decided to suspend completely the *Discipline*'s entire section on slavery for the states south of Virginia. (Virginia was part of a conference that included Maryland and Pennsylvania, and hence as such its conference—if not Virginia herself— was more congenial to emancipation.) Consequently the Methodist Episcopal church printed two editions of its *Discipline*, northern and southern versions. The process of compromise was essentially completed by 1808, when the General Conference fatefully decided to allow "each annual [local] conference to form [its] own regulations, relative to buying and selling slaves."

Although other slight changes were made in the ensuing decades, by 1808 the Methodist retreat on emancipation was virtually completed. Francis Asbury summed up the Methodist position, and the reasoning behind it, in

February 1809 while attending the Virginia Conference: "Would not an *amelioration* in the condition and treatment of slaves have produced more practical good to the poor Africans, than any attempt at their *emancipation?* The state of society, unhappily, does not admit of this: besides, the blacks are deprived of the means of instruction; who will take the pains to lead them into the way of salvation, and watch over them that they may not stray, but the Methodists? . . . What is personal liberty of the African which he may abuse, to the salvation of his soul; how may it be compared?"

Since the first Methodist circuits were not established in Kentucky until 1786, and since not until the Great Revival was Methodism of much influence in Kentucky, Methodist views on slavery there were predetermined by the events outlined above. Nevertheless, many individual Methodist ministers maintained their commitment to abolitionism despite the *Discipline's* revisions. The Reverend John Ray, active in the state in the mid-1790s, "would seldom lodge at the house of a slaveholder. . . . when invited home with a stranger, his prompt interrogatory would be: 'Have you any Negroes?'" He asked the same question of all prospective Methodist preachers. Benjamin Lakin, another itinerant, two decades later bemoaned "the curse of Negro slavery" and confided to his journal, "If there is Justice in the universe, does not the blood of these people cry for vengeance, and will not God soon avenge their cause on their oppressors?" Peter Cartwright was an outspoken critic of slavery and eventually left Kentucky for Illinois because he found the slaveholding society repugnant to his principles and restrictive of his activities.

Cartwright, who was never very sensitive to those whose opinions differed from his, bluntly characterized those Methodists who compromised with slavery as giving in to social and economic expediency. Such an indictment was more true of Methodist laymen than of the ministers. Clearly as the Methodist church underwent its enormous expansion in the South, becoming with the Baptist church the dominant denominations of the region, it adjusted to local situations. It was the Methodists' ability to adapt to the mores of the people that made possible their growth.

But something more profound was at work than mere succumbing to economic opportunism. The Methodist preachers, like all the southern evangelicals, never developed a feeling of societal responsibility for their secular communities. In fact, the only community toward which they felt a responsibility was their congregation. They conceived their obligations to be almost entirely spiritual, and their focus was on the individual sinner of either race within their congregational communities. When they attacked sins, they spoke of personal sins that conversion could cure. While worldly reform was good in itself, when it threatened their highest duty it must be relegated to a secondary level. What had the slaves gained if the Methodists, because of their abolitionism, were prevented from showing them the path to eternity? Would not the Methodists be woefully remiss if they let their concern for a *civil* relation prevent their making available to southern sinners of both races the Good News? The Methodists in good conscience made a moral compromise wherein the reality of their situation demanded only two possibilities: be a sacrosanct minority that might very well die out in the South in pursuit of emancipation, or be the vanguard of the gospel adjusted somewhat to the region, hoping all the while that suasion could, if not end slavery, ameliorate it and Christianize the slaves. The decision afforded no easy choice.

Because the Kentucky Baptists were not part of a nationwide association, each congregation was autonomous. Congregations could and did form local associations, but the absence of an overall superintending body provided more leeway for individual and congregational independence. Baptist emancipationists could withstand local public opposition and, free of any adjudicative organization above, form separate abolitionist churches. Because the Baptists, like the Methodists, began as a denomination primarily of the poor and nonslaveholding people and because they too were pietistically opposed to materialism and speculation, the Baptists' freedom from external supervision allowed their period of antislavery activity a longer existence. Yet in a slave society, the ultimate impact of Baptist emancipatory views was limited.

The majority of Kentucky Baptists had emigrated from Virginia and kept up a ministerial correspondence with their colleagues in the Old Dominion. Kentucky Baptists were then soon aware of the resolution passed by the Virginia Baptists in the General Committee of April 1789: "*Resolved,* that slavery is a violent deprivation of the rights of nature, and inconsistent with a Republican Government, and therefore recommend it to our brethren, to make use of every legal measure to extirpate this horrid evil from the land, and pray Almighty God that our honorable legislature, may have it in their power to proclaim the great jubilee, consistent with the principles of good policy." Although the conservative nature of this statement is indicated by the last phrase, antislavery ideas took root among Kentucky Baptists who had sent messengers to the Virginia meeting.

Hardly had the abolitionist sentiment reached Kentucky before the Rolling Fork Baptist Church, in Nelson County, sent a query to the Salem Association convening in early October 1789. "Is it lawful in the sight of God," it asked, "for a member of Christ's Church to keep his fellow creature in perpetual slavery?" The association, recognizing the controversial nature of the query, cautiously replied: "The Association judges it improper to enter into so important and critical a matter, at present." Rolling Fork, led by Joshua Carman, an emancipationist, was dismayed by this response. After several years of agitation within the Salem Association, Rolling Fork withdrew from the association in 1796 and became for a few years an independent emancipatory church. Mill Creek Church had also withdrawn from the Salem Association in 1796 for the same reasons. Two years earlier Josiah Dodge, another Baptist emancipationist, along with Joshua Carman had persuaded several members of the Cox's Creek, Cedar Creek, and Lick Creek Baptist churches also to withdraw from communion with slaveholders, and the combined members constituted a new church near Bardstown about 1794, probably the first emancipatory church organized in Kentucky. Within a few years this small group of independent churches attracted other Baptist emancipationists, men such as David Barrow, the venerable William Hickman, and the publicist Carter Tarrant. The few antislavery proponents constantly faced opposition and frustration, but they kept their position alive in Kentucky.

Often the clergy were far more liberal in their views than were the laity. For example, the Elkhorn Baptist Association in August 1791 appointed a committee of three (all of whom were emancipationists) to draw up a report on slavery. The report, emphatically antislavery, was approved by those at the association meeting, but the individual churches constituting the association were displeased by the report. An extra session of the association was called to consider the matter, and the association, bowing to popular pressure, officially disapproved the "memorial" on "the Abolition of Slavery."

The gradual withdrawal of antislavery Baptists into a separate organization must be seen in the context of bitter opposition. While several individual congregations followed the lead of abolitionist ministers, the associations which were made up of the bulk of Baptist congregations were pressured into support of the status quo. For that reason the Elkhorn Association in August 1805, after receiving numerous queries regarding slavery, finally announced that "This Association Judges it improper for ministers Churches or Association to meddle with emancipation from slavery or any other political Subject and as such we advise ministers and Churches to have nothing to do therewith in their religious Capacities." This was a public rebuke to those who entertained an antislavery position, and some individuals voluntarily withdrew from the association. That same year the North District Association subjected David Barrow to a harsh questioning of his views, and when many of the churches were unsatisfied with his answers, he was charged in 1806 with "preaching the doctrines of emancipation to the hurt and injury of the brotherhood." When Barrow refused to compromise his principles, he was excluded from membership by the North District Association.

The conservative pressure for avoiding all controversial political topics like slavery was intense. Ministers such as Carter Tarrant (1806) and William Hickman (1807) were forced to resign from their churches and, in the words of Tarrant, were "hunted and driven from [our] obscure retreats, (by a kind of crusading inquisition)." Moreover, antislavery ministers were ostracized by the majority. The Salt River Church asked its association for advice: "Is it consistent with good order for Baptist Churches of our union to invite those preachers to preach among us, that have withdrawn from among us, on account of slavery?" The answer it received was: "It is considered imprudent (under present state of things) to intermeddle therewith." It was such associational ostracism and repression which forced Baptist emancipationists to form separate antislavery churches. By so doing they became isolated, their views were quarantined, and their influence on the rest of society effectively limited. But as an autonomous association of abolitionist Baptists, they have been often cited as evidence of the strength of antislavery opinion among early Kentucky Baptists. Their courageous survival does indicate the tenacity of their principles, but more importantly, their small numbers point up the overwhelming strength of proslavery sentiment.

Evicted from membership in the existing Baptist associations, expelled from their membership (and sometimes pastorates) in the existing churches, the Baptist advocates of antislavery met in conference in August 1807 to consider their future. Eleven ministers and nineteen laymen were present and, in response to various queries, made firm their commitment to ending slavery. The following month they met again and organized themselves into a society with the unlikely name of "The Baptized Licking-Locust Association, Friends of Humanity." (Licking-Locust was an antislavery Baptist church near the Ohio River.) Made up mostly of churches in the northeastern part of Kentucky, they differed from other Baptists only in their views on slavery. The tenor of their statements of principle betrays their essential conservative nature and suggests the kind of conservative arguments they faced. Their letter to the churches in union with them, written September 1807, summarizes their position against slavery and shows how unjustly they perceived themselves to have been treated by the Baptist establishment. Tarrant's pamphlet *Substance of a Discourse Delivered in . . . Versailles . . . 1806* carefully refuted the charges against them by showing that they neither usurped the civil power nor tempted slaves to rebellion.

The Baptized Licking-Locust Association, Friends of Humanity, had been in existence only a year when they resolved "that the present mode of Associations or confederation of churches was unscriptural, and ought to be laid aside." They then organized themselves into a more secular group, the Kentucky Abolition Society. The emancipatory Baptist churches continued as autonomous bodies, but their overt antislavery activities were now channeled through the Abolition Society. In 1811 David Benedict, who traveled to Kentucky in pursuit of his research, computed that while there were 17,511 Baptists in Kentucky, only twelve churches, twelve ministers, and 300 laymen were emancipationists. And as Benedict concluded, "there is such a strong current against the emancipation of slaves, and custom, covetousness, indolence, and ambition, find so many arguments in favor of slavery, that there seems but little prospect, that any material change will at present be effected."

Although composed primarily of Baptists, the Kentucky Abolition Society attracted persons from all persuasions. Probably never consisting of more than several hundred members, it actively promoted its reform views. Believing, as its constitution stated, that "Slavery is a system of oppression, pregnant with moral, national and domestic evils, ruinous to national tranquility, honor and enjoyment, and which every good man wishes to be abolished, could such abolition take place upon a plan which would be honorable to the state, safe to the citizen and salutary to the slaves," the society carefully avoided radical stances. Its purposes were declared to be: "To pursue such measures as would tend to the final constitutional abolition of slavery" and "the domestic slave trade," and in the meantime "to look after the interests of free Negroes and mulattoes," to "ameliorate the condition of slaves," to seek justice for those blacks illegally held in bondage, and to speak out against slavery.

By so clearly accepting the constitutional restraints of the state, the society tried to avoid charges of irresponsibility, but at the same time it minimized the possibility of effecting real change. No doubt the society was more sanguine about its ability to achieve reform by way of a temperate policy than we might deem justifiable from hindsight, but what else could it realistically have done? Shortly after the society was founded, Carter Tarrant, the president, wrote to the prestigious Pennsylvania Society for the Abolition of Slavery asking for counsel, remarking that "we who have been brought up among the horrors of slavery have made but poor proficiency in the principles of humanity." The first advice cautioned: "We have considered the interests of the blacks best promoted by moderation in our requests in their behalf and by unremitted endeavours to change publick opinion in their favour, other than by too warm an opposition to strengthen the prejudices, and increase the rancour of our opponents. The result has been the rapid diminution of personal slavery in this state with the certain assurance of its intire [sic] extinction in a very short time." But that was in Pennsylvania. The situation was far more explosive in Kentucky, and, as the stated purposes of the Kentucky Abolition Society suggest, the inability to promote appreciably either abolition of slavery or the domestic slave trade left no alternative but practical amelioration. It periodically denied in any way agitating among slaves or fomenting servile insurrection. This ultimately was the outcome of most southern abolitionist efforts: they were transformed into ameliorative reforms which ironically were used by proslavery proponents to refute the charges of northern abolitionists that slaveowners abused their slaves.

By all odds the most influential and outspoken Baptist emancipationist was David Barrow, who wrote a hard-hitting pamphlet, *Involuntary, Unmerited, Perpetual, Absolute, Hereditary Slavery, Examined; on the Principles of Nature, Reason, Justice, Policy, and Scripture* (Lexington, Ky., 1808)—the fruit of a "cool and impartial examination of nearly thirty years." He contemptuously dismissed "high toned republicans . . . swaggering in our public assemblies . . . talking loudly in favour of *Liberty!*" who nevertheless owned slaves, and his refutation of the biblical defense of slavery glowed with scorn. Yet even this gnarled veteran of abolitionist controversy carefully leavened his radical demeanor with an irenic aside that made clear he believed in gradual emancipation which provided ample time for slaves to be prepared for freedom so that the end of slavery would "give no shock to the community." Thus was early abolitionist radicalism transmuted into circumspect reform.

Despite opposition the tiny Kentucky Abolition Society tenaciously struggled on. Because the regular press was largely closed to the society, it decided to expand its activities. In May 1822, with the Reverend John Finley Crowe, a Presbyterian, at the editorial helm, it began publishing a monthly newspaper, the *Abolition Intelligencer and Missionary Messenger*. (At this time there was but one other abolitionist newspaper in the nation, Benjamin Lundy's *The Genius of Universal Emancipation*, published briefly in Tennessee and after 1824 in Baltimore.) Yet this courageous attempt to spread abolitionist views lasted only a year, and in April 1823, with less than four hundred subscribers in Tennessee and Kentucky, the newspaper folded. By 1827 the Kentucky Abolition Society, whose membership had dwindled below two hundred, went out of existence. Those Kentuckians still committed to emancipation were soon organizing relatively uncontroversial state chapters of the American Colonization Society, the first auxiliary having been formed in Kentucky in 1823 and the second in 1827.

Such then was the final outcome of religious antislavery in Kentucky—one movement for ameliorating the conditions of slaves, another, often related, movement to transport emancipated slaves and free blacks to Africa. Though every denomination occasionally went on record in support of improving the living conditions of slaves and providing them with religious instruction, perhaps none more consistently advocated amelioration than the Episcopalians. Such a policy of uncontroversial reform complemented the essentially conservative nature of the church. From the 1830s to the Civil War, various Episcopal clergy conducted well-attended (and closely supervised) Sunday schools for slaves, often teaching them to read so they could study the Bible themselves. Special religious services were held on Sunday afternoons; slaves were baptized, married, confirmed, and buried; their physical well-being was consistently advocated. Amelioration was often seen as preparatory to colonization. Examples of such religious concern could be chosen from all the denominations.

Opposition to the slave trade remained strong and widespread, but slavery was firmly ensconced in Kentucky society. The colonization movement proved to be of little moment. Many whites gave it theoretical support, and for a time it seemed an idea whose time had come. But the growth of the colonization movement represented a departure from the earlier abolitionist societies whose spokesmen were usually opposed to slavery and occasionally hoped to improve the condition of blacks themselves. The colonization movement was primarily proslavery and antiblack, though the few remaining true abolitionists usually joined it as the only route open to reform. Free blacks were an anomaly in the southern slave society, and hence the drive to remove them enjoyed widespread political and religious support. Although some of the bolder antislavery proponents tried to use the colonization society as a vehicle for emancipation, the predominant attitude was revealed in December 1828 when the Kentucky State Colonization Society was organized for the purpose of relieving the state of "the serious inconveniences resulting from the existence among them, of a rapidly increasing number of free persons of colour, who are not subject to the restraints of slavery."

Nevertheless, most Kentuckians supported colonization only in the abstract, and blacks understandably hesitated to leave their kin and migrate to an Africa that was unknown. The various denominations gave some verbal support—after all, colonization would remove the "free people of colour" who could be a threat to white safety and a temptation to slaves. Yet few funds were ever raised. Abolition sentiment swelled briefly in the 1830s, then subsided. Opposition to James K. Birney's short-lived Kentucky Antislavery Society in Danville forced him to leave the state. There simply was no significant support for actually abolishing slavery. As one advocate of antislavery wrote, after chronicling how religious spokesmen over the years had retreated from their earlier moral opposition to slavery to an unwillingness to disturb mere civil relations: "My conclusions are, that every order and condition of society among us, with a few individual exceptions, are for letting things alone."

In the mid-1840s the colonization movement again caught fire temporarily, and the Kentucky auxiliary of the American Colonization Society even purchased a forty-square-mile tract of land in Liberia and named it "Kentucky in Liberia" with its capital city designated "Clay Ashland." A ship was chartered in early 1846 to transport black immigrants to Africa, but only thirty-five left Kentucky. Despite scattered church support, especially from the more affluent Presbyterians, the colonization movement never flourished. It was, in fact, only by cultivating a stance of studied obscurity and remaining uncontroversial that the colonization societies were able to linger. Only a bare trickle of Kentucky blacks returned to their ancestral homeland.

No simple conclusions can be drawn on the result of religiously inspired antislavery in Kentucky; indeed, the very term antislavery includes a spectrum of activities ranging from radical abolitionism to conservative amelioration and colonization. Nevertheless, the impact of Kentucky antislavery cannot be casually dismissed. Partly because of the heritage of David Rice, David Barrow, and the "Friends of Humanity," Kentucky throughout the antebellum era was unique to the South in its relative freedom to discuss critically the peculiar institution. During the 1830s and 1840s in particular it seemed to be expected that some young clergy and college-trained men would entertain cautiously critical attitudes. Powerful family connections also often allowed one to speak out in the face of popular support of slavery. There was in fact an abortive movement in 1849 to provide for abolition in the new state constitution. Yet even the supporters of the emancipatory clause very conservatively intended to colonize the freedmen. Emancipationist hopes were temporarily lifted when the constitutional convention approved a declaration critical of slavery in the abstract. But despite such an indictment, the new state constitution, ratified May 1850, not only protected slavery but actually made emancipation more difficult than before.

Though individuals in Kentucky had unusual freedom to converse on abolition, their plans remained abstract and unfulfilled. Perhaps the emancipationists never seriously believed their ideas were capable of being realized in a slave society. That such thought was allowed expression suggests the relative liberality of Kentucky and indicates that the system of slavery there was much less harsh than elsewhere. Certainly the tradition of religious antislavery contributed to this phenomenon. And yet the pernicious effects of slave society did closely confine abolitionist activities; practical means to effect real change were discouraged or curtailed; and abolitionism remained a chimerical idea. Those who could not accept such ultimate restraints—people like Birney—were either forced or chose to leave. Kentucky antislavery was not able to effect emancipation, but it did materially contribute to the kind of climate from which Kentucky unionist sentiment developed. In the face of both open and subtle opposition, in spite of almost certain failure, a flicker of antislavery sentiment persisted in the Bluegrass State. And when the momentous choice was forced in 1861, Kentucky chose loyalty to the Union in a war that ultimately ended slavery. Surely the heritage of religiously inspired antislavery was involved in many individual moral decisions that kept Kentucky in the Union.

7

THE
RELIGIOUS CULTURE

IT IS ADMITTEDLY very difficult to gauge the pervasiveness or intensity of religious beliefs in any society, particularly one in the past. On the merely descriptive level, Kentucky impressed many contemporary observers as a religious area. In what purported to be a fair-minded traveler's guide to a number of midwestern states and territories, Samuel R. Brown wrote, "It is a solemn truth, that religion is no where more respected, than in Kentucky." A more critical observer, speaking of Lexington in particular, told his readers that "if the people have any striking defect, it consists in the fact that they are subject to sudden and violent excitements both in religious and political affairs." And still another, more intimate glimpse into religion was offered by Daniel Drake, who, in a conventionally sentimental pen sketch of his mother, lovingly related that though "she was still more illiterate than my father, [she] was pious, and could read the Bible, Rippon's hymns, and Pilgrim's Progress. Her natural understanding was tolerable only, but she comprehended the principles of domestic and Christian duty, and sought to inculcate them. This she did never by protracted lectures, but mixed them up with all our daily labors." It was this infusion of religion into the humdrum affairs of everyday life that gave Kentucky society its religious cast.

The Christian faith strongly influenced the way persons viewed proper conduct, acceptable attitudes, and ultimate goals in life. That slavery, for example, was both defended and attacked by reference to scripture illustrates the tendency to seek religious justification for the society's beliefs and behavior. To be a member of any of the varied communities—kinship, congregational, occupational, professional—that together constituted Kentucky society, one could not flout anti-Christian beliefs. Even to be religiously liberal, much less a doubter or deist, was to court extreme disfavor with one's neighbors. Clearly religion was a major component in the self-identity of Kentuckians both individually and collectively. What had emerged was a religious culture.

Consider what church membership offered to early Kentuckians. Here, gathered together, would be welcome faces sharing the same beliefs and spiritual goals, a community of faith. A number of rituals emphasized the concept of the group fused together into a body of believers—the Lord's Supper was a major sacrament, and it powerfully symbolized the unity of the members under the fatherhood of God. Baptism; occasionally foot washing; the kiss of charity or love; the right hand of fellowship; calling each other Brother Jones or Sister Polly; jointly singing the tunes lined out by the minister or clerk; these and other rites drew people together and gave individualistic, independent-minded pioneers a sense of community. Walking or riding on horseback through miles of forests, then coming to the small wooden church with its familiar ceremonies and its congregation as company to relieve the usual loneliness, the early settlers must have approached Sunday church services with great anticipation.

Religious services were a vital force in pioneer life. Persons identified themselves with a particular church, and membership, ceremonialized through baptism and communion, brought a variety of benefits. Fellow members cared for one another in sickness or hardship. They united for joint projects from barn raisings to log-rollings to constructing a new church. Death was ever near, and the church with its promise of eternal life and comforting support was always ready to offer both hope and help. Couples met, courted, married, lived by, and died within the physical and spiritual confines of their church.

The intellectual life of the plain folk centered in the church. In an age when most people had no recourse to books, periodicals, or newspapers, the church with the Scriptures as source provided the only abstract ideas most persons ever experienced. The congregations were amazingly democratic. Not only did all members, men and women, blacks and whites, vote on church matters, but they also discussed and decided such theological issues as the concept of the Trinity and the nature of Atonement.

The tenets of their faith were preached in simple, vivid language, using such homely illustrations and analogies that listeners could feel the heat of hell and luxuriate in the joys of heaven. The sermon theology was unsophisticated, but so were the hearers, and the popular churches spoke the common man's language because they knew their audiences. The Presbyterians tried to maintain educational requirements for their ministers, but many of the successful Baptist and Methodist exhorters, who during the week were farmers, had an education grounded more in faith than in learning. Vigorous preaching, combined with hymns whose verses and refrains expressed simple theological maxims in easily memorized form, taught generations of Kentuckians a religious faith that pervaded their lives, even when they could not live up to the church's expectations.

The social attractions of church membership are clear. In the early days of settlement, as hundreds of individuals and families were breaking away from their home communities in Maryland, Virginia, or the Carolinas and pushing westward, loneliness and homesickness were nagging companions. Often lodged in rude, isolated cabins, pioneer families sought through church membership to re-create what they most missed, the familiarity of old customs and beliefs. The poignant desire for community that made many Kentuckians so eager for church growth and revival was the result as much of a feeling of social dislocation as of a feeling of spiritual estrangement from God. The social sources for a need to recapture the warmth and sense of belonging associated with church membership—to be part of a church family with all the sense of mutual support and love implied by the term—lent a special aura of authenticity to the articulated desires for God to send a revival. It was a deep-seated belief that the congregational form was right, as confirmed by scripture, tradition, and common sense, that gave a religious dimension to the social pressures for church membership. These forces blended into a powerful urge that revealed itself most memorably in the organizational success of the Great Revival when church rolls expanded tremendously.

Religion is a difficult concept to define; at the most abstract level, it is a series of symbols which help explain the world and give meaning to life. In addition to shaping a person's comprehension of his society, religious symbols, because they carry with them certain values and truths which must be realized in the believer's life-style, help shape how a person responds to his world. Clearly the social environment, as *perceived* by the believer, influences his behavior. For that reason the economic, social, political, and demographic factors which impinge upon the believer must be considered in the context of his religious perspective. It is no surprise that ministers would attempt to interpret in religious terms the ultimate causes of social strains immediately caused by rapid shifts in population. Their religious interpretation in turn would result in a plan of action to solve the root cause.

126

The Great Revival of 1800, which was expected and prepared for in the aftermath of what seemed an era of crisis, is a good example of this cultural phenomenon. There is then a subtle relationship between theological ideas, social conditions, and religious actions, a relationship often illustrated by history.

In the dark of the early morning of December 16, 1811, the southwestern portion of Kentucky was jarred by a massive earthquake which, centered near New Madrid, Missouri, shook the whole mid-Mississippi valley. The ground heaved, flatboats were ripped away from their moorings, huge fissures gaped open, lakes instantly appeared, the Mississippi River itself seemed to stop flowing momentarily and slightly changed its course. Two more severe shocks came, on January 23 and February 7, 1812, and perhaps as many as 1,800 lesser tremors quivered the region in the three months following the first quake. The inhabitants of the disturbed area were understandably frightened. Many instantly assumed the end of the world had come, while others huddled together in churches, praying for divine deliverance. Some who had lived indifferent to religion were now "crying out for mercy." As one contemporary, Jacob Bower, recorded: "I expected immediate destruction, had no hope of seeing the dawn of another day. Eternity, oh Eternity was just at hand, and all of us unprepared. . . . The people relinquished all kinds of labour for a time, except feeding stock, and eat only enough to support nature a few days. Visiting from house to house, going to meeting, Singing—praying, exorting, and once in a while ketch a sermon from a travelling Minister. Men, Women, and children, everywhere were heard enquiering what they must do to be saved. This shaking continued more or less for near two years, sometimes just perceivable. Deists & Universalists in those days were scarce." Bower himself was converted and became a Baptist preacher.

Revivals erupted in most churches, and apostates among these "shaking Christians" were said to be no more numerous than among other revival converts. The Western Conference of the Methodist church alone recorded a 50 percent increase in 1812. Baptists and Presbyterians shared in the harvest. Such a reaction to a frightening mystery is predictable. The frontiersmen with no scientific training, seeking an explanation for the tremors, turned to supernatural causes. God was either signaling the end of time or expressing his divine wrath for sinners' unbelief; the obvious response to either was implicit in the religious explanation: flee to God for deliverance and salvation. The result was a resounding revival.

Another natural disaster that led to a revival was the terrible cholera epidemic which struck Lexington in the summer of 1833. Robert Davidson, the Presbyterian chronicler, has left a vivid firsthand account which reveals the terror and mystery spawned by the pestilence:

The year 1833 was memorable on account of the awful ravages of that formidable epidemic, capricious in its march, inscrutable in its features, and baffling the resources of the medical art, the Asiatic Cholera. . . . Early in June, 1833, the epidemic made its appearance, and filled every house with mourning. In the short space of nine days, fifteen hundred persons were prostrated, and dying at the rate of fifty a day. . . . Within a fortnight it was computed that about five hundred persons fell victims, notwithstanding half the population had fled at an early period. The panic was terrible. . . . The streets were deserted. The marketplace was desolate. . . . The graveyards were choked. Coffins were laid down at the gates by the score, in confused heaps.

When the epidemic lifted, the survivors seemed "stunned and stupefied." But as those who had fled returned to resume normal life, they had to try to come to terms with what had happened. God had allowed the disaster to occur as a way to teach people a lesson, to warn them powerfully of the danger of living unconverted lives. It was through a religious perspective that people found some purpose, a glimmer of hope, in the onslaught, and correspondingly their religious outlook led to a resurgence of piety. During 1834 all the churches of Lexington—Episcopal, Baptist, Methodist, Presbyterian, Catholic—enjoyed a revival in which hundreds joined while many more had their faith invigorated. One of the functions of religion, then, is to provide people with a positive way of accepting adversity.

Clearly most revivals do not spring from such drastic events as earthquakes or epidemics. Usually they emerge from a period of religious retrenchment when for a variety of reasons religion seems declining and on the defensive. Just such a season of slackness, punctuated with some talk of Unitarianism and "Infidelity" near Lexington, led to a Presbyterian revival in 1828–1829; similar conditions also produced a simultaneous Baptist revival. As clerical observers noted the efficacy of concerted periods of intense prayer and frequent preaching for gaining converts, the revival was gradually transformed from a mysterious work of God showered upon chastised Christians into a technique, a method used by practical-minded though praying leaders to produce multiple conversions.

Camp meetings were still common among the Methodists, but they too had been restrained, regularized, and in effect institutionalized. They were now held at appointed times on grounds specially prepared for the services. The Baptists and Presbyterians, who on the whole now frowned upon camp meetings, increasingly turned to what was called the "protracted meeting" after the 1828–1829 revival. At first the meetings lasted three to four days, but they were soon extended to two full weeks. The protracted meetings were widely advertised; groups of clergy cooperated to handle the rounds of prayer, preaching, and singing. A typical day consisted of "a Prayer-Meeting at sunrise; an Inquiry Meeting, for the serious and anxious, at nine o'clock; and preaching at the usual hours, morning, afternoon and evening." The use of specialized "Revival Preachers" arose in conjunction with the protracted meetings. Such new measures laid the foundation for steady church growth. Previously membership would rise spectacularly during a revival, then level off or even decline slightly for a decade or so until the next revival. The regularly scheduled annual camp meeting or protracted meeting meant churches were augmented yearly.

Revivals were now "held," not sent by God (though, of course, it was felt God sanctioned their use). Individuals still believed that God provided the grace which made salvation possible; persons still approached God individually and believed he heard their prayers and their cries and through the mediation of Jesus Christ offered salvation. But the arena of this activity had become rationalized; churches put on revivals expecting God to provide his "services" if they did the fieldwork. Certainly the technique—despite the opposition of antimission Baptists who opposed the presumption of "aiding" God's work—brought greatly increased church growth to Kentucky. Baptist membership, for example, tripled between 1820 and 1860.

Religion in antebellum Kentucky extended from the churches into all other aspects of life. This permeation constituted the religious culture, and it was religious discipline that impressed religious values throughout the culture. All the popular churches had methods of dealing with infractions of the moral rules. The Baptist churches held monthly business meetings on Saturdays. A major portion of their time was spent on discipline. Witnesses to a member's alleged infraction testified; the accused was next heard from; witnesses were cross-examined; and the members then acted as a church court to determine guilt or innocence. In the case of guilt, the transgressor either asked for and received pardon upon promise of good behavior or was expelled from the church. The Methodists used their class meetings to oversee conduct. Because itinerant ministers were often not present, elders supervised weekly class meetings in which gospel lessons were taught, hymns sung, and discipline maintained. The Presbyterians formally used the meetings of the presbytery as the first jurisdiction for behavioral problems, though in practice individual ministers in their sermons preparing the congregation for communion (what was called "fencing the table") chastised those who had done, or said, or presumably even thought wrongly. The Catholics, of course, prescribed Confession as a means of discipline and repentance.

A substantial portion of church records relates the problems of discipline, and they show a remarkable democracy of effort. Both sexes, both races, all classes were called to the bar of moral justice. Hardly any aspect of life was left unwatched; church records show persons disciplined for profanity, drunkenness, heresy, inattendance at church, working or traveling on Sunday, mistreating slaves, beating their wives, fornication, adultery, gambling, horse racing, attending the theater, joining the Masons, overcharging, and so forth ad infinitum. Persons within a congregational community were expected to settle all disputes among themselves in the church court, without recourse to secular courts. Clearly, the workaday life, not simply Sundays, was touched by one's faith. That people voluntarily submitted to such a system suggests the powerful role religion then played. Church discipline also provided a moral escape valve, allowing transgressors in a high-voltage religious culture to atone for their sins and, with congregational forgiveness and acceptance regained, resume their lives at peace with themselves and their neighbors. In the intervals between cathartic revivals, discipline ministered to personal wrongdoing.

Discipline was not at all mere punishment, it was "watch care." Fellow members would help persons avoid moral mistakes, help guide them through difficult problems. In a way, church discipline was an early form of group counseling. Together the religious community could work out answers to the ethical dilemmas that many individuals—not just the accused—might encounter. What could have been a rigidly strict system was usually moderated by common sense and kindness. As an early Baptist congregation wrote in its covenant, "We do agree to watch over one another, to Reprove and admonish one another in Charity and Brotherly love as ordered by Christ in the Gospel."

The Kentucky churches constantly had troubles arising from the sale and use of whiskey. The drinking of drams and toddies was almost universal in early Kentucky. A supply of whiskey was considered as essential to a household as sugar and salt; offering a neighbor or visitor a drink was as common as sharing coffee today. Whiskey became almost a medium of exchange; even ministers' salaries were paid in gallons. Ministers drank, mostly in moderation, sometimes operated stills, and sold whiskey as they might corn or tobacco. No social stigma was attached to drinking; only gross inebriation was frowned upon. And it was this personal vice of drunkenness that attracted church attention.

The church records of all groups show a recurring and universal struggle against the sin of drunkenness. Ministers themselves were occasionally reprimanded and suspended for overdrinking. The Baptists seem to have been particularly concerned with inebriation, for Baptist members were cited repeatedly for drinking to excess. The Methodists since the days of Wesley had been ardent foes of John Barleycorn. Drunkenness, however, was a national problem, and the American Temperance Society was organized in New York in 1828. Within two years, a Baptist minister, Alva Wood, helped organize and was chosen president of the first Kentucky temperance group, called the Fayette County Temperance Society. Other church bodies—except the antimission Baptists who opposed all reform or revival movements and as such were labeled "Whiskey Baptists"—supported the cause of temperance, despite some public opposition. The making of bourbon was, after all, big business in Kentucky. In the early 1840s the Washingtonian movement, an enthusiastic temperance crusade, found numerous supporters. Later the Sons of Temperance and still later the Independent Order of Good Templars spread the gospel of abstinence, at first hoping suasion alone could control drinking. But when that seemed not to work, they increasingly turned to the idea of legal prohibition.

After the Maine Liquor Law passed in 1851, temperance promoters across the nation called upon their legislators to outlaw alcoholic beverages. Kentucky churchmen, including the Disciples of Christ, threw their support to this new plan; the General Association of Baptists in Kentucky even formally advocated prohibition. Nevertheless, prohibition was not enacted, and though Baptist concern persisted, the vogue of temperance waned. This was the major evangelical movement for secular reform, having far more support than the emancipation movement, yet it was couched in religious terms. Alcoholism was seen as the personal problem of individuals, not as a symptom of larger social problems. As such, temperance in Kentucky remained limited in its scope and promise.

Kentucky churches gingerly supported several other reforms which were popular outside the South, but in the Bluegrass State all reform was localized, individualistic, and oriented toward religious rather than secular institutions. The churches on the whole avoided political questions. The Presbyterians led in the move to organize Sunday schools, with the Methodists and Baptists holding back because of their slight suspicion of learning and the belief on the part of the antimission Baptists that Sunday schools interfered with God's work. The state's first Sunday school was apparently opened in "Liberty Hall," the Frankfort home of Mrs. John Brown. She had persuaded a local Presbyterian minister, Michael Arthur, to devote an hour on Sundays to catechizing the children and teaching them Bible lessons. There was also limited success in organizing auxiliaries of the American Bible

Society in Kentucky. The Lexington Female Bible Society, for example, conducted a house-to-house campaign, but in the course of a year distributed only twenty-eight Bibles and ninety-three New Testaments. In the mid-1840s, after a reform-minded director revolutionized patient care at the pioneering Kentucky Lunatic Asylum, chaplains and religious services were provided for the patients, and religion was even considered by the asylum's director to be potentially curative.

Another example of very limited reform was the Baptist affiliation with the Kentucky Choctaw Academy. Congressman Richard M. Johnson (later Martin Van Buren's vice president) was a large landowner in Scott County and a member of the Great Crossings Baptist Church. Johnson was desperately in need of money, so when in 1819 the federal government began providing funds for Indian education, he saw his opportunity. Using his political clout, he obtained permission to open a federally funded Indian school on his property, and using his religious connection with the local Baptist church, he persuaded the church to provide a missionary outreach to the Indians. Thus the Johnson Indian School opened. The Indians learned some vocational skills, the local Baptists spread the gospel, and Johnson reaped the profits from the federal largess of $6,000 annually. Johnson did sincerely believe in both vocational and religious education for the Indians, and he induced the Baptist Board of Foreign Missions to supervise the operation of the school. A number of the Indians subsequently joined the Great Crossings Baptist Church, and three even became missionaries to their people farther west. The school had a maximum enrollment of ninety-eight and continued with its nominal Baptist control until 1842.

The seemingly innocuous issue of home missions—missions to destitute areas of the United States—became one of the great controversies in Kentucky religion. During the first two decades of the nineteenth century, almost no criticism was directed toward missions. The Transylvania Presbytery, for example, resolved to aid in the gathering of mission funds, and regular missionary sermons were preached before collections were taken. The Methodists heartily supported local efforts to extend the gospel circuits of their itinerants. Even among the Baptists there were, in 1816, no less than six missionary societies in Kentucky. But this era of good feeling proved short-lived. As national benevolent societies were formed—such as the American Tract Society, American Bible Society, American Home Mission Society, and American Sunday School Union—with headquarters in Boston, New York, or Philadelphia, leadership was drawn primarily from a northeastern Congregational and Presbyterian elite. Using modern bureaucratic techniques, the mission societies took on a character alien to Kentuckians and Southerners in general.

The response of the southern churches to what they perceived as outside intervention tells much about both the South and her churches. One way they reacted was to pull away gradually from national ecclesiastical organizations and form regionally distinct church bodies such as the Methodist Episcopal Church, South, and the Southern Baptist Convention. The other, less common but far more extreme way, was the southern antimission movement led by the so-called Hard-Shell or Primitive Baptists. Some antimission sentiment no doubt tinctured the larger groups' drawing apart, but antimissionism was primarily a minority movement led in Kentucky by the most rural Baptists located in the mountainous northeastern portion of the state. Living isolated from the commercial forces that were transforming the North, and isolated even from most of the growth and prosperity of Kentucky, these backwater Baptists clung desperately to their traditional faith. They would brook interference with neither their way of living nor their way of believing. Outside missionary agents were to them descending hordes of money-hungry cultural interlopers. Their existence, separate from the larger settlements of Kentucky, made them extremely provincial, defensive, and tenacious in support of their life-style. They read the Bible in ultraliteralist fashion, accepting only what they believed the Bible commanded. The Scriptures did not explicitly authorize Sunday schools, seminaries, tract societies, or missions; thus they opposed all as being unscriptural. They rejected missions on sociocultural grounds as an invasion of their bailiwick and on theological grounds as a newfangled human invention.

The three leading proponents of antimissionism were all Baptists, John Taylor, Daniel Parker, and Alexander Campbell. John Taylor, a pioneer Kentucky minister, was incensed at the missionaries' presumption that there was no real religion in the West. He took this as a condemnation of the people in general and the old-time preachers in particular. Taylor guarded carefully the autonomy of the local congregations, and he feared the national bureaucracy of the mission movement would destroy grassroots control. He published his views in a slashing pamphlet, *Thoughts on Missions* (1820), whose vividly memorable phraseology plagued missionaries for decades. Even more of an enemy of missions was Daniel Parker, who preached near the border of Kentucky and Tennessee. He pushed Taylor's arguments further in his own pamphlet, *A Public Address to the Baptist Society* (1820). Four years later this was reprinted, and another was published on the same subject. Since God was supreme, Parker argued, his church did not need the human support of various agencies and societies. Taking this idea to its logical end, Parker wrote that even to promote revivals and Sunday schools was worse than presumptuous, it was sheer folly because the lost could not be saved despite all the preaching in the world. In a pamphlet published in 1826 Parker outlined his Two-Seed-in-the-Spirit doctrine, a kind of extreme predestinarianism combined with primitive Manicheism. People born of the good seed—an emanation from God—were

already saved, and those born of the evil seed—an emanation from Satan through Eve—were children of the devil
and thus irredeemably bound for hell. Human effort was
irrelevant. The other great mission opponent was Alexander Campbell, who while still in his Baptist phase
ridiculed missions in his newspaper, the *Christian Baptist,* censuring them for their alleged greed and cultural
imperialism.

The antimission or Primitive Baptists remained a small
minority; in 1843, when there were 59,302 regular Baptists in Kentucky, there were but 7,877 of the antimission
breed. In 1890 throughout the South there were 45,000
Hard-Shells, and 1,125,892 missionary Baptists. Yet the
Hard-Shell views poisoned the well of Baptist cooperation for years. They constantly attacked the Baptist majority for promoting local societies, protracted meetings,
and so forth. The antimission body, rural and isolated
from the mainstream of Kentucky life, saw time passing
them by and reacted by clutching their threatened culture more tightly. From their religious perspective, the
status quo represented the good and the godly, while
change meant not only loss but degeneration. Their response was one of aggressive reactionism wherein their
way of life was defended with religious fervor, for indeed,
their religious culture was at stake. On an interpretative
level, the antimission Baptists are important because
they were an intense microcosm of the larger Baptist—
and southern—society. As their remote mountain valley
communities were to the rest of Kentucky, so the rural,
agricultural South was to the rapidly changing, urban-
izing, industrializing North with its shifting views on
slavery. Much of southern history may be seen as a
religiocultural reaction to the emergent North.

In response to changing realities and attitudes in the
North, particularly the growing strength of abolitionism,
the major southern denominations felt their way of worship and life threatened. Separation was their answer to
save their "purer" faith and "higher" civilization.

By the early 1830s the national Presbyterian church was beginning to split apart. Two factions had arisen, the New School group centered in New York and New England, and the Old School group which was strongest in the South. The New School Presbyterians, liberals both in theology and in reform, were becoming strongly proabolition. Moreover, they controlled such agencies as the American Home Mission Society. More conservative Presbyterians throughout the Union differed with them on their theological innovations, but it was the southern Presbyterians who were most affected. The antislavery pronouncements of many New School spokesmen scandalized southern clergy. Looking at the growing abolition sentiment in the New School synods of Ohio, western New York, and Pennsylvania, one observer wrote, "It looks as if the Presbyterian Church were becoming an Abolition Society." Clearly, as a committee of Old School Presbyterians chaired by Robert J. Breckinridge of Kentucky reported, "Our people are no longer one body of Christians." Increasingly disturbed by the doctrinal and radical views of the New School, southern Presbyterians moved to take over the General Assembly, attending in large numbers in 1837. With western support the Old School had a majority at the General Assembly and thus abrogated the old Plan of Union with Congregationalists and attacked the American Home Missionary Society (AHMS) and the American Education Society. At the 1838 assembly New School delegates came in great numbers, determined to reassert their control. The result of the head-on collision was the organization of two general assemblies, the South dominating the Old School one. After 1838 there existed what was in effect two Presbyterian churches, northern and southern. By withdrawing their group from the national organization, southern Presbyterians could avoid theological innovation, abolitionist sentiment, and the generally antisouthern outlook of the AHMS missionaries. Consequently southern Presbyterianism grew more conservative and more supportive of southern folkways.

The Methodist church was similarly split over slavery. After the truce had been worked out by 1808 in which southern slaveowners could be Methodists without having their labor system interfered with, southern Methodism grew rapidly. Until the early 1840s Southerners in fact dominated the Methodist church. But as abolitionism flourished, many in the North left Methodism to join other denominations less respectful of southern sensibilities. Northern bishops began to relax their rule, allowing local Methodist conferences to express their emerging abolitionist sentiment. This prevented the draining away of Methodist emancipationists, but it was to cause trouble in the South. By the time the General Conference met in 1844, the antislavery forces held the balance of power. When the General Conference decisively upheld the suspension of a Baltimore Conference minister for refusing to free his slaves, southern Methodists knew the die was cast. Northern radicals, they believed, had taken control. As one delegate remarked, "the great question of unity is settled, division is inevitable."

The breaking point came several weeks later when Bishop James O. Andrew of Georgia was ordered to cease his official duties as long as he did not free the several slaves he owned via marriage and gifts—and since Georgia law prevented their manumission, Andrew's only alternatives were to resign or fight. He chose combat; the southern delegates supported his decision; the northern delegates would not back down. The conference voted against Andrew, though all but one southern delegate backed him. Tempers flared, and on June 3 Bishop William Capers of South Carolina offered a series of resolutions providing for a sectional separation. A committee of nine subsequently issued a report, the Plan of Separation, spelling out how the division would take place and preventing either group from organizing churches in the territory of the other. Then the fateful

1844 General Conference adjourned, but the next day the southern delegates agreed to call a convention for the following May in Louisville. Meeting there on May 1, 1845, the delegates voted overwhelmingly to separate formally from the Methodist Episcopal Church and form another body, the Methodist Episcopal Church, South. The southern Methodist church, now freed from any liberalizing tendencies, became even more adjusted to the social and racial customs of its region and more identified with the southern way of life.

The Baptist church was also split into sectional camps. For years the completely autonomous Baptist congregations had organized themselves into local and regional associations, convening every three years in a national Triennial Convention. Thus there was a loose connection into a national Baptist church. Then in April 1840 there was organized in New York City the American Baptist Anti-Slavery Convention which promptly drafted "An Address to Southern Baptists." Southern Baptists instantly read the handwriting on the wall: they assumed subsequent triennial conventions would subject southern delegates to adverse criticism. Shortly before the 1844 convention "A Southern Baptist" published a pamphlet entitled *A Calm Appeal to Southern Baptists, in Advocacy of Separation from the North in All the Works of Christian Benevolence.* He argued that Northerners dominated the boards of the various benevolent societies and that the token southern representatives were mere "spectators." At the 1844 convention, therefore, the Georgia Baptist Convention in a test case recommended that a slaveholding preacher, James E. Reeves, be appointed a missionary by the Board of the Home Mission Society. The appointment was refused. The southern associations then withdrew from the Home Mission Society and formed a Board of Domestic Missions supported and controlled by Baptists in the South. Relationships between southern Baptists and the national organizations grew more troubled. Soon there was a strong sentiment for completely breaking away from the Triennial Convention. Consequently on May 8, 1845, in Augusta, Georgia, 377 enthusiastic delegates from eight southern states and the District of Columbia met and organized the Southern Baptist Convention. Soon they formed a southern Foreign Mission Board and a Home Mission Board and poured thousands of dollars into these agencies. Like the Methodists and the Presbyterians, there now existed a distinct southern Baptist church which identified itself totally with the regional mores.

The majority of Kentucky Baptists, friendly to missions in principle though opposed to northern-dominated societies, were avid supporters both of the Southern Baptist Convention and its regionally controlled missions. The previously organized "Roberts Fund and China Mission Association," headquartered in Louisville, continued to underwrite the missionary labors of Issachar J. Roberts in China, though after 1845 it operated virtually as an auxiliary of the Foreign Mission Board in Richmond. In 1851 it was completely absorbed by the Foreign Mission Board and ceased its independent existence. The antimission Baptist minority was opposed even to the Southern Baptist Convention.

So the Kentucky Baptists did as most southern churchmen did: they simply withdrew from cooperation in national movements and formed local organizations over which they had control. The three dominant religious bodies of the South had thus seceded from the national churches by 1845, presaging the Confederacy. Each denomination strongly justified its action by reference to its duty to the slaves. If the denomination remained affiliated with increasingly abolitionist national agencies, slaveholders, suspecting the churches of possible emancipationist tendencies, would surely limit their freedom to preach to blacks. Thus southern churchmen reasoned that their religious responsibilities to their slaves required their breaking away to remove any suspicion that they might endanger southern institutions. Partly to respond to sincerely felt duty and partly to refute abolitionist statements that southern churches callously neglected the spiritual needs of the blacks, there was a remarkable increase in white church missions to the slaves after the mid-1840s. Both the separation and the slave mission aided the growth of southern self-righteousness; the breaking of the national religious cords only made political secession easier. The ties that bind had broken.

But how did southern religion become so intertwined with southern folkways as to become identified with, indeed defined by, southern society? To answer that provocative question, one must look more carefully at the theology preached and believed in the South. The dominant theology of the South was conversion-centered. To win over sinners was the highest aim of most ministers, and conversion, followed by a pietistic emphasis on personal behavior, was the desired Christian goal. Individuals were primarily concerned with their own sins, not society's. Theirs was a faith that urged denial of the values of this world and pointed instead to a preoccupation with the next. One's secular station in this life was deemed unimportant. Such a religion was obviously well suited to the great majority of white Southerners who represented the broad middle class between slaves and proud planters. It offered contentment with their earthly status, promised a better life to come, and thereby infused even the most monotonous and dreary existence with the hope to persevere. As such, the antimission Baptists to the contrary, southern evangelical orthodoxy ministered against class antagonism.

The conversion emphasis was not one to elicit social criticism. Instead, the tendency of southern religion was toward an acceptance of the existing social arrangements. The thrust of the religion was inward, not outward; being "saved" meant primarily a stance of being, rather than doing. Christians had entered a state of forgiveness in which relief from sin and guilt was found. One's earthly life was in a sense thus irrelevant to the condition of being forgiven—note the Baptist belief that "once saved, always saved." Social responsibilities could be shunted aside as one inwardly "grew in grace." Individuals—and by extrapolation the society—were enabled to make progress toward perfection through the institutionalized mechanisms of church discipline and especially the annual revival, which offered release from the burden of sin. Quite possibly the pervasive southern guilt about slaveowning, which inflicted even those spokesmen who defended slavery as the class structure undergirding southern civilization, made necessary a regional religion providing highly visible and ritualized escapes from guilt—revivalism. The existence of slavery thus contributed to the whites' desire, even need, for many churches, and the existence of many churches with their untainted orthodoxy and their annual revivals was considered proof the region was particularly religious. Southerners apotheosized what they termed the South's Christian civilization. Southern Christians, southern churches, and even southern society were deemed special, more Christian than other parts of the nation. Ironically the southern churches with their individualistic, conversion-centered theology ended up sanctifying the status quo and legitimating the "southern way of life."

What has been termed the "affirmation of southern perfection" was thus in important respects an outgrowth of southern religiosity. And this religion swung to support the South as the region came into conflict with national norms. As the North expanded and became urbanized, the South comparatively stood still. The rest of the nation developed cities, industry, and a commercial, booster spirit, and slaveholding became more and more an embarrassment, a besmirchment of national principles. North and South grew farther apart, intensifying southern sectionalism and threatening the South's traditional culture. As a consequence regional spokesmen became aggressively defensive of the southern way of life. The passive traditional society became self-consciously conservative, and the conservatism evolved into a dynamic cause. Because southern life appeared particularly Christian to those churchmen whose theology allowed them to overlook the social evil of slavery, threats against the South were interpreted as threats against the last remaining stronghold of Christian civilization. The religious values had so interpenetrated the southern way of life that a hybrid culture had developed, the religious culture later known as the Bible Belt.

This self-consciously "sacred" sectionalism was intense in the Deep South. Kentucky as a border state, with her populous northern region tied into the national commercial market system, was just enough removed from the rural isolationism of the Deep South to harbor strong Unionist sentiments. Her greatest political leaders from Henry Clay on had been southern Unionists. However, the southwestern portion of Kentucky, with more cotton and slaves, was strongly secessionist. With feelings almost equally divided, Kentucky tried to maintain an uneasy neutrality. It was not until the Confederate army invaded the state in September 1861 that Kentucky officially supported the Union side. But many Kentuckians still sentimentally favored the Confederacy. While some 75,000 Kentuckians joined the Union army, perhaps 35,000 fought in the Confederate army. As has been written, "the hearts of a majority probably were with the South, but their heads were with the North." What had helped capture the hearts of the people was evangelical religion, which permitted them to transform their slaveholding society into a religiously justified "superior civilization." As one Kentuckian had written in futile support of secession, a southern nation could "clothe the world with our staple—give wings to her commerce, and supply with bread the starving operative in other lands, and at the same time preserve an institution that has done more to civilize and Christianize the heathen than all human agencies besides—an institution alike beneficial to both races, ameliorating the moral, physical, and intellectual condition of the one and giving wealth and happiness to the other." Slavery set the South apart, but Southerners perceived their peculiar institution within a religious culture that enabled them to find moral purpose in it. As such, evangelical religion contributed mightily to southern self-consciousness and southern sectionalism. And it was the presence in Kentucky of this religious culture that, after the war, made Kentuckians strongly pro-Confederate and pro-South. The Myth of the Lost Cause was in large measure an outgrowth of southern religion.

Bibliographical Note

THE FIRST THREE chapters of this book draw heavily from my previous work, *The Great Revival, 1787–1805: The Origins of the Southern Evangelical Mind* (Lexington, Ky., 1972), which contains an extensive bibliography. Inquiring readers may find there most of my sources, supplemented by Walter B. Posey's *Frontier Missions: A History of Religion West of the Southern Appalachians to 1861* (Lexington, Ky., 1966). I have also found helpful Frances Keller Swinford and Rebecca Smith Lee, *The Great Elm Tree: Heritage of the Episcopal Diocese of Lexington* (Lexington, Ky., 1969).

Indispensable for the story of Kentucky Catholicism are the following: Sister Mary Ramona Mattingly, *The Catholic Church on the Kentucky Frontier, 1785–1812* (Washington, D.C., 1936); J. Herman Schauinger, *Cathedrals in the Wilderness* (Milwaukee, 1952), and *Stephen T. Badin: Priest in the Wilderness* (Milwaukee, 1956); Thomas Spalding, *Martin John Spalding* (Washington, D.C., 1973); and Martin John Spalding's early account, *Sketches of the Early Catholic Missions of Kentucky* (Louisville, [1844]). Very useful for background are Joseph William Ruane, *The Beginnings of the Society of St. Sulpice in the United States, 1791–1829* (Washington, D.C., 1935); Gilbert J. Garraghan, *The Jesuits of the Middle United States*, 3 vols. (New York, 1938); Robert Frederick Trisco, *The Holy See and the Nascent Church in the Middle United States, 1826–1850* (Rome, 1962); and Sister Agnes Geraldine McGann, *Nativism in Kentucky to 1860* (Washington, D.C., 1944). The older biographies of the leading figures should also be consulted,

146

such works as Camillus P. Maes, *The Life of Rev. Charles Nerinckx* (Cincinnati, 1880); Victor F. O'Daniel, *The Right Rev. Edward Dominic Fenwick* (Washington, D.C., 1920); and Sister Columbia Fox, *The Life of the Right Reverend John Baptist Mary David* (New York, 1925). A particularly important article is Francis X. Curran, "The Jesuits in Kentucky, 1831–1846," *Mid-America* 35 (October 1953):223–46.

Much of what I say about slave religion is based on rather obscure primary sources. I will here indicate some of the more readily available works that influenced my interpretation; occasionally my views represent a rejection of much of the recent literature. On the issue of Africanisms surviving in America, see Melville J. Herskovitts, *The Myth of the Negro Past* (Boston, 1941), and John S. Mbiti, *African Religions and Philosophy* (Garden City, N.Y., 1970). Interviews with elderly Kentucky slaves may be found in George P. Rawick, ed., *The American Slave: A Composite Autobiography,* 19 vols. (Westport, Conn., 1972), vol. 16. On slavery in Kentucky see Ivan E. McDougle, *Slavery in Kentucky, 1792–1865* (Westport, Conn., 1970; original ed., 1918), and J. Winston Coleman, Jr., *Slavery Times in Kentucky* (Chapel Hill, N.C., 1940). The historiography of American slavery is extensive, but the general reader may begin with two recent studies, John W. Blassingame, *The Slave Community: Plantation Life in the Ante-Bellum South* (New York, 1972), and Eugene D. Genovese, *Roll, Jordan Roll: The World the Slaves Made* (New York, 1974). Recent works on slave religion include Genovese's *Roll, Jordan Roll;* Henry H. Mitchell, *Black Belief* (New York, 1975); James H. Cone, *The Spirituals and the Blues* (New York, 1972); Gayraud S. Wilmore, *Black Religion and Black Radicalism: An Examination of the Black Experience in Religion* (Garden City, N.Y., 1973); and Milton C. Sernett, *Black Religion and American Evangelicalism: White Protestants, Plantation Missions, and the Flowering of Negro Christianity* (Metuchen, N.J., 1975).

For white antislavery, David Brion Davis provides ample context in *The Problem of Slavery in the Age of Revolution, 1770–1823* (Ithaca, N.Y., 1975). Most of the material in my chapter 6 came from scattered primary sources; the reader may, however, consult with profit Donald G. Mathews, *Slavery and Methodism: A Chapter in American Morality, 1780–1845* (Princeton, 1965); H. Shelton Smith, *In His Image, But . . . Racism in Southern Religion* (Durham, N.C., 1972); and Asa Earl Martin, *The Anti-Slavery Movement in Kentucky Prior to 1850* (Louisville, 1918). Similarly chapter 7 is drawn from a wide variety of sources. Articles and books that have helped shape my viewpoint are Clifford Geertz, "Religion as a Cultural System," in *Anthropological Approaches to the Study of Religion*, ed. M. Banton (London, 1966), pp. 1–46; Bertram Wyatt-Brown, "The Antimission Movement in the Jacksonian South: A Study of Regional Folk Culture," *Journal of Southern History* 36 (November 1970):501–29; and Samuel S. Hill, Jr., *Religion and the Solid South* (Nashville, 1972). See also chapter 12 of my *The Great Revival*, cited above. The *Filson Club Quarterly* and the *Register of the Kentucky Historical Society* have printed many significant articles over the years; students should consult these journals for all aspects of Kentucky history.